# EMPOWERING SPIRIT WISDOM

## A Warrior of Light's Guide on Love, Career and the Spirit World

### Kevin Hunter

Warrior of Light Press
Los Angeles, California

Copyright © 2014 Kevin Hunter.

All rights reserved. No part of this book may be used or reproduced by any means, graphic, electronic, or mechanical, including photocopying, recording, taping or by any information storage retrieval system without the written permission of the publisher except in the case of brief quotations embodied in critical articles and reviews.

The author of this book does not dispense medical advice or prescribe the use of any technique as a form of treatment for physical, emotional, or medical problems without the advice of a physician, either directly or indirectly. The intent of the author is only to offer information of a general nature to help you in your quest for emotional and spiritual well-being. In the event, you use any of the information in this book for yourself, which is your constitutional right, the author and the publisher assume no responsibility for your actions.

Warrior of Light Press
www.kevin-hunter.com

Body, Mind & Spirit/Angels & Guides
Inspiration & Personal Growth
Spirit Writing. Channeling (Spiritualism). Spiritual life.

PRODUCTION CREDITS:
Project Editor: James Szopo

All rights reserved. Copyright © 2014
ISBN-10: 0615966470
ISBN-13: 978-0615966472

# Acknowledgements

Thank you to my spiritual posse that consists of God and my personal sports team of Angels, Guides, Archangels and Saints.

# Chapters

**CHAPTER 1**
The Soul, Spirit and Power of the Light _____1

**CHAPTER 2**
School for Human Souls and the Hell Dimension _____8
   Painting with God _____14

**CHAPTER 3**
Musings About Connecting with the Spirit World _____16

**CHAPTER 4**
Law of Attraction _____27
   Visualizing Your Reality _____29
   Thoughts Produce Circumstances _____30
   Daydream _____32
   Money, Success, Abundance _____34
   Manifesting _____36

**CHAPTER 5**
Transform Your Work Life _____39

**CHAPTER 6**
Disconnecting and Eliminating _____49
   Stay Away From Noise _____50
   Full Moon Releasing _____52
   Flowers _____53
   Your Light is Power _____55

## CHAPTER 7
The Power of Love and Relationships _____ 57
    Messages on Love _____ 59
    Chemistry _____ 63
    Invite Love Into Your Life _____ 67

## CHAPTER 8
The Secrets to Successful Relationships _____ 73

## CHAPTER 9
Stages of Coupledom _____ 79
    Dating _____ 80
    Casually Dating Vs. Exclusively Dating _____ 83
    Boyfriend or Girlfriend _____ 84
    Relationship _____ 85
    Marriage, Civil Union, Commitment _____ 90

## CHAPTER 10
Random Messages from Spirit _____ 92
    Power of Prayer _____ 93
    The Ego's Wrath _____ 95
    Shielding _____ 98
    Cord Cutting _____ 100
    Take Care of Your Body _____ 101
    Dancing and Singing _____ 103
    Halloween _____ 105
    Rainbows _____ 106
    Twin Flame Love _____ 107

## CHAPTER 11
Messages from the Archangels _____110
   Messages from Archangel Michael _____112
   Messages from Archangel Raphael _____116
   Messages from Archangel Gabriel _____118
   Messages from Archangel Uriel _____120
   Messages from Archangel Nathaniel _____123
   Messages from Archangel Jophiel _____126
   Messages from Archangel Raziel _____131
   Messages from Archangel Ariel _____133
   Messages from Archangel Haniel _____137
   Messages from Archangel Azrael _____142
   Messages from Archangel Metatron _____145
   Messages from Archangel Sandalphon _____148
   Messages from Archangel Raguel _____150
   Messages from Archangel Chamuel _____155
   Messages from Archangel Zadkiel _____160
   Messages from Archangel Jeremiel _____164

Jesus Christ and Mother Teresa _____167

# Introduction

After the release of my book, *Warrior of Light: Messages from my Guides and Angels*, I received an abundant amount of positive notes from readers who were asking additional questions for answers that were not in that book. They asked if I had any other similar books with additional information. This is where *Empowering Spirit Wisdom* came to light. *Empowering Spirit Wisdom* is focused on the more practical. It's broken up into several parts or sections. Chapters 1-3 are focused on the soul, spirit and ego. Chapters 4-6 are geared towards ones work life, soul vibration and manifesting. Chapters 7-9 are my favorite chapters as they focus on love and relationships. Chapter 10 covers random additional or highlighted spirit messages. This is concluded with Chapter 11, which is the longest chapter in the book devoted to practical messages for everyday life concerns from some of the prominent Archangels.

*Empowering Spirit Wisdom* is the follow up greatest hits book to *Warrior of Light: Messages from my Guides and Angels*. The other *Warrior of Light* books include, *Realm of the Wise One, Darkness of Ego* and *Reaching for the Warrior Within*. The content in *Warrior of Light, Empowering Spirit Wisdom* and *Darkness of Ego* are sporadically disbursed in a series of *Warrior of Light* mini-books called, *Spirit Guides and Angels, Soul Mates and Twin Flames, Divine Messages for Humanity, Raising Your Vibration,* and *Connecting with the Archangels.*

# Author's Note

All of the *Warrior of Light* books are infused with practical messages and guidance that my Spirit team has taught and shared with me revolving around many different topics. The main goal is to fine tune your body, mind and soul. This improves humanity one person at a time. You are a Divine communicator and perfectly adjusted and capable of receiving messages from Heaven. This is for your benefit in order to live a happier, richer life. It is your individual responsibility to respect yourself and this planet while on your journey here.

The messages and information enclosed in this and all of the *Warrior of Light* books may be in my own words, but they do not come from me. They come from God, the Holy Spirit, my Spirit team of guides, angels and sometimes certain Archangels and Saints. I am merely the liaison or messenger in delivering and interpreting the intentions of what they wish to communicate. They love that I talk about them and share this stuff as it gets other people to work with them too!

There is one main hierarchy Saint who works with me leading the pack. His name is Nathaniel. He is often brutally truthful and forceful, as he does not mince words. There may be topics in this and my other books that might bother you or make you uncomfortable. He asks that you examine the underlying cause of this discomfort and come to terms with the fear attached. He cuts right to the heart of humanity without apology. I have learned quite a bit from him while adopting his ideology, which is Heaven's philosophy as a whole.

I am one with the Holy Spirit and have many Spirit Guides and Angels around me. As my connections to the other side grew to be daily over the course of my life, more of them joined in behind the others. I have often seen, sensed, heard and been privy to the dozens of magnificent lights that crowd around me on occasion.

If I use the word "He" when pertaining to God, this does not mean that I am advocating that he is a male. Simply replace the word, "He" with one you are comfortable using to identify God for you to be. This goes for any gender I use as examples. When I say, "spirit team", I am referring to a team of 'Guides and Angels'. The purpose of the Warrior of Light books is to empower and help you improve yourself, your life and humanity as a whole. It does not matter if you are a beginner or well versed in the subject matter. There may be something that reminds you of something you already know or something that you were unaware of. We all have much to share with one another, as we are all one in the end. This book and all of the *Warrior of Light* series of books contain information and directions on how to reach the place where you can be a fine tuned instrument to receive your own messages from your own Spirit team.

Some of my personal stories are infused and sprinkled in the books. This is in order for you to see how it works effectively for me. With some of my methods, I hope that you gain insight, knowledge or inspiration. It may prompt you to recall incidents where you were receiving heavenly messages in your own life. There are helpful ways that you can improve your existence and have a connection with Heaven throughout this book. Doing so will greatly transform yourself in all ways allowing you to attract wonderful circumstances at higher levels and live a happier more content life.

~ Kevin Hunter

# Chapter One

## THE SOUL, SPIRIT AND POWER OF THE LIGHT

God created everything that exists in the Universe and all of the parallel Universes. Some say that you are born in the likeness of His image. They are not far off because you branched out of Him. There are sparks of Light that shoot out of His presence. It looks like the kind of white sparklers that you might see in a firework, but there is an abundant amount of this Light shooting out of Him. These sparklers of Light are the individual souls born and formed out of God. This is why you are born with the greatest qualities of God. Those qualities consist of 100% pure, unconditional love, joy and peace. You are born into a human body in this complete state. Unfortunately, all human souls house the human ego. The human ego tampers with your development as you age in a human body. It teaches you to hate, harm and hurt the planet and each other. It teaches you to experience negative emotional traits such as fear, guilt, stress, depression, anger and low self esteem. This creates a wide array of issues that wreak havoc on your existence in this life. It is the biggest cause of turmoil and upset on the planet.

God is magnificent beyond human comprehension. His Light is vast spreading like a gigantic blanket that fills up every atom and cell that exists in any spiritual plane. He resides within every living thing, person, planets, or organism. He is in the trees, in the mountains, in the beaches and deserts. There is no escape from Him. There are Archangels, Saints, Spirit Guides and Angels who reside in other dimensions as well. They know everything about you from your thoughts and feelings, to what is coming up ahead for you. Many of them can be everywhere at once. Imagine what God is like if He is more powerfully prophetic than any other creation or entity in the Universe? There are ten core spirit dimensions. The first seven are the numerous stages of where human souls go to. Most move into the fourth after the Earth dimension. The higher the number of that dimension, then the closer God is. God is everywhere, but He is even more powerful and present in the higher dimensions. Dimensions eight through ten are filled with legions of Archangels, Saints or Ascended Masters.

God would never hurt a soul. They are His Children after all. He would never ask you to hurt or harm another soul either. Those who do this and protest that it is in the name of God do not know God by this act. You know God when you exude love. All souls must develop, grow and evolve. They do this by going to school. This is similar to how earthly souls go to grade school as a child in order to learn something and make something of their lives. This school is on a much larger scale than this. This particular school or class begins when your soul is born into a human body to live an Earthly life. Human souls are on Earth in human form for countless reasons. One of them is to learn lessons in order to develop and grow their individual souls. There are also higher evolved souls born into a human body in order to act as teachers. Many of them come from various spirit realms on the other side. They are the ones teaching humanity about love. Other evolved souls who elected to live an Earthly life are the ones teaching others about love and compassion. They are the ones righting a wrong. If those souls did not choose to incarnate into a human body for an Earthly life, then life on Earth would blow up into an even bigger chaos than it already has. They contribute to keeping it somewhat contained and on the straight and narrow. There are also souls born into human form who take care of God's planet. This is part of how some souls contribute positively in the name of God. He expects everyone to display His best qualities, which are what you already have within you, even if you have forgotten how to access it. This includes love, joy, peace and compassion. This is what a high vibrational state of being is. In my book, *Realm of the Wise One*, I discuss how to recognize some of the higher evolved souls that exist on the planet. They are the ones making positive contributions to the betterment of humanity or the planet in some way. The Wise Ones are typically the teachers. They have an inner sense of knowing. Part of this is due to the many lifetimes they've lived on Earth.

All human souls have an ego which expands once your soul enters a human body in the Earth's dense atmosphere. The reason for this is much like a test. You are not taking the kinds of tests you would take in school, but you have other kinds of tests to take. These are tests where you learn lessons that enhance and grow your soul so that you can be a most magnificent soul. When your soul enhances and grows, then your light grows big, bright and more powerful. This is what attracts positive circumstances in your Earthly life too!

The brightest lights in human souls are those who display high vibration traits. They are also the Children around the world. This is until some Children develop negative traits learned from their peers, community and adults. This dims the light within their soul causing them to exude negative traits that have repercussions throughout their Earthly life. Some of those repercussions include attracting in a continuing array of challenging circumstances. Karma is built up due to bad behavior and must be paid back. No soul is going to get away with murder in the end. This Karma is paid back in this lifetime or future lifetimes when you are asked to incarnate repeatedly until the Karma has been balanced and your soul has evolved to a great degree.

The human body you occupy will reach a point where it will expire. This is no secret as every human soul is accustomed to this reality. It might be one of the few things that all human souls can agree on. There is no real death and end. It is only the beginning. Your soul exits the body it was born into. The light of your soul expands as it crosses over to the other side. This is also when your soul begins increasing and expanding gradually to perfection. This is where you remember the lessons you learned in your Earthly life which prompt you to become a brighter soul because of it. It is important to note that your ego will still be intact. What this means is that if you were an irritating nag on Earth, then you will carry this trait as you cross over. After you cross over, then you begin working on diminishing the negative traits you adopted on Earth. This is why working on all parts of you now is essential. Where you head to after this life has no space or purpose for any of the nasty habits that you adopted while living an Earthly life. Nasty habits are what your ego collects at this time as if it has value. It is corrupt and destructive aligning itself with the Devil. Your ego is the real monster and Devil at play here.

Take care of this planet and everything God created in it. Put a stop to the volatile destruction of your inner self and its surroundings. This cripples and harms other human souls merely to feed your ego, which has no worth or power in the end. When you head back home to the other side everything you attempted to gain disintegrates. Wake up and take your soul's existence seriously. Humanity as a whole has become a spoiled, greedy, materialistic movement. It is time to rise above this weakened ego driven mentality. This, *kill or be killed,* notion that there is not enough to go around, or that you are better than someone else will crumble when you leave the body you inhabit. Always remember to revert to love in order to experience peace.

*Saint Nathaniel's message
interpreted by the author:*

When you have fulfilled your lessons and life purpose, then you will get to go back home. Home is a much grander paradise than life on Earth. When you understand this reality, you learn that none of this ego based hate filled hunger matters. You cannot take anything or anyone you've crossed paths with for granted. They all play an important part in the process of your soul's growth experience. It has nothing to do with the body you consume which enables you to live an Earthly life. You inhabit the space of the body in order to move around in what might seem to be an intricate design. See the false reality that this is not real in the way you identify your life to be. As a collective, all souls have advanced in the sense that they have made this Earthly life somewhat of a functional place to endure. However, it is not your home base in the end. It is merely one long adventure in a school. Once you've completed this Earthly life run, you get to go home and talk about what you were lucky enough to learn while on Earth. What your Spirit team of Guides and Angels on the other side will ask you is, how about love? Did you remember to love? Did you mend and forgive the Karmic relationships you intended to do? Or will you need to endure another long period of time before you both agree to meet up in a future Earth life to complete the cycle?

You created some wonderful technology to function with one another, but your lower selves have taken advantage of it by treating it with disrespect. This is done in the same manner a child would when it is newly in human form. It reacts to things innocently and naively stomps out of turn. This child grows up to exude that same personality trait acting the way it did in lifetimes past. We wait for you to break the cycle that your soul endures through one life after another.

There are other similar realities to the Earth reality

running in other parallel universes. We know this might sound like science fiction. Science fiction is what you have put in your Earthly entertainment designed to bring you joy while you function on Earth. This science fiction is not fiction at all, but stems from what some souls have seen in your mind's eye. Those who do are what you consider to be a star child or person. They are souls who come from world's different from yours, and yet you discredit that this can be true. All souls are psychic beyond comprehension. Human ego takes over and diminishes those telecommunication receptors with us. Every now and then you receive what others call a hit of clairvoyance. You see in your mind's eye the lives you once lived in other dimensions. What you're really doing is communicating with us accurately. We communicate with you so that you can remember who you are as a soul, and know what is important on your Earthly journey. We made this challenging for you, yet so many of you are evolving rapidly and strengthening your soul in this process. Indeed you have opened up to the other realities that exist beyond your current soul lesson. We watch many souls growing and teaching others about Heaven. Ignoring those who express doubt and remembering that you are not truly home. You will be home soon when you cross over. Remembering to walk the path of the light will assist you in many great ways. The Light will ease the burdens, turmoil and grief you often experience. Call upon us to awaken your soul and assist you down the right path. Bathe in His love and strength, which wipes those negative troubles away. All is well we always say. This is to remind you that there is no reason to suffer when you are living in the Light. The Light protects you from the evil you sometimes face.

There are different levels and branches of souls living an Earthly life. There are advanced souls in human form sent to teach you a wide range of soul enhancing gifts. All of the teachings lead to the same goal, which is love. Love is the thought form that began when God consummated. His love is overpowering since He is in every molecule, atom and cell.

You cannot escape him.  You cannot lie or cheat.  You cannot deny Him.  He is undeniable.  He knows what you were thinking of yesterday and where you will be tomorrow.  He knows when you will head back home to Heaven.  He knows what you will be doing before that time.  He knows what you agreed to do when you entered an Earthly life.  He knows when you have strayed from this agreement.  When you've strayed beyond comprehension or He sees you have given up, then He pulls your soul out of your temporary body.  You are delivered back home to Heaven.  You know in that instant what you neglected to do while living an Earthly life.  You wish you had this epiphany when you were on Earth and are amazed at how effortlessly it comes to you in Heaven.  While living an Earthly life, connecting with us will assist you on staying on the right course.  This is so that you do not stray too far from your goal and purpose.  This goal is where the true happiness you search for resides.

# Chapter Two

## School for Human Souls and the Hell Dimension

Why would God create human souls to begin with? Why create Lights that are destructive and hateful to one another? The following chapter is what God, Saint Nathaniel and his team of disciples have relayed on this.

*Saint Nathaniel's message
interpreted by the author:*

God knows all souls are highly spiritual at their core, even if they do not remember being in this state. He knows who your soul was before you entered an Earthly life. He knows those qualities were diminished due to society's conditioning. He sees your soul as pure innocence and love. This was the state you were born in. He understands that because He gave you free will choice wiping your memory clean when you were born into a human life, that you will do and say things that are not of God. It is intended that you learn to grow and evolve even if it takes many lifetimes. He knows human souls will act out in fear or naivety. This happens when you do not understand the concept of what and who you are in truth. You are taught and led by others on how to function on Earth. This is someone else's moral compass which is generally ego. It has no basis in real reality. You must reach spiritual evolvement by branching out into independence and figuring it out for yourself. Some will experience an awakening when they reach a certain human age. This awakening will help you remember who you were before you were born. Many human souls are blocked and embedded richly in the material world. They remain blocked at the same level they were when they were Children. They will repeat another lifetime until they come to the profound realization of spiritual reality.

Human ego convinces the soul that you are less than you are. When your soul came into a human life, you were perfect in every way. You become less than when you allow your ego full control over you. You move into this state when you allow your material world to influence your actions. This heavy attraction to material superficiality stunts your soul's growth. None of the gadgets and material items that have been created to entertain you will have any validity beyond keeping you entranced and pre-occupied in a timewaster. This contributes to delaying your soul's growth and purpose. It is okay to enjoy yourself pending that it is not in addictive ways that stop you from moving forward. This is not for anyone's benefit, but your own.

God created souls out of His Light. Your human body is a temporary vessel you inhabit for the sake of an Earthly life experience filled with lessons and growth. An Earthly life is the bottom of the barrel so to speak. It is the lowest level as far as spiritual advancement goes in all of the spirit dimensions. It was designed for brand new souls to go to "school" in order to learn and gain knowledge. However, God and spirit also send highly evolved souls to have an Earthly life in order to act as teachers, healers, and leaders. The evolved soul agrees to this mission, even if they temporarily forget while living an Earthly life. They incarnate in a human body in order to coach and inspire chosen souls who are ready to move to the next level on their soul's growth. These evolved or evolving souls agreed to come into an Earthly life for this purpose. The human souls that have allowed their ego to run their show and influence them poorly are in great need of these teachers. They may come into contact with these evolved souls, but may not likely be aware of it since their ego is in full control. They are lost in the chaos and negativity that their lower mind creates. Eventually there is a point with some of them when they reach rock bottom and are in desperate need of guidance or answers. They are ready to receive in this state and therefore the right teacher for their soul's growth will appear.

You witness negativity, darkness and violence around you and ask why would God waste His time? His creation is not destroying each other as it would seem. Because that is impossible since your soul is eternal. The harm these particular souls cause are only harmful in ways that is understood on the physical Earth plane. He gave you free will so that you can learn what is right from wrong. The Earthly life is one made up of students. They are the new souls who are much like children that act out in a tantrum. The other souls are the teachers who enlighten and empower in a myriad of positive ways. There are vast reasons placed on each individual as to why they are having an Earthly life. This is one that must be gained on your own time.

This Earthly life school for souls is similar to how humankind has created schools around the world to educate you on the ways of functioning in current human life. Unfortunately, they rarely include spiritual or godly studies. The one reason humankind exists in the first place is exempt from these studies. There is little to no teachings of love and compassion for all of humanity. This is what spiritual and godly studies are. This is partly due to those who make decisions in the human school system have long forgotten who they are as a soul. Some human souls grow angry if the word God is uttered in the human life education system. This is also due to the rise of a belief of non-belief gained through society's programming and human life development on Earth. You are allowed to set up life as you see fit in order to feel comfortable, safe, and secure. These are humankind needs, but not real soul needs. It is much like chasing a mirage for comfort when the relief, safety and security you crave lies closer than you would believe. These needs are achieved by connecting with the one true Divine source. This contentment lives within each human soul. It is a part of God who supplies all of your needs when you request. God allows humankind to act how they please. This includes using His name in vain, as well as causing hate crimes, destruction and violence. Those that act out in this manner cause negative Karma, which they will have to pay back. This might take them lifetime after lifetime until they figure out that their actions are harmful and not of God. God is all about love.

There is a dimension in existence where the souls who are buried underneath masses amount of ego such as eternal hate, destruction, anger and bitterness reside in. It's a dense atmosphere similar to the dimension that Earth exists. It is no place for any soul to inhabit and we call it the 'dark dimension'. These souls are not cast there, but their soul moves into that plane willingly. Those particular souls are attracted to false desires and interests. They are the souls who choose to suffer over peace. They choose to be self-sabotaging or self-destructive while living an Earthly life. They are the souls that hurt others while living on Earth. This might have been done through violence or prolonged hate with no sign of remorse and rebirth. They might have been a soul who caused love pain to other souls they came into contact with. This could also be someone who repeatedly abandons a love mate for selfish needs and priorities.

The souls in this dark dimension have very little love in their hearts beyond what they expect in return from others. They have an insatiable need and desire for the toxic material comforts they craved while living an Earthly life. The dark dimension is the least evolved above the Earth plane. They are recognizable on Earth as they are also the ones who display negative traits on a daily basis. They consume themselves with greed and chase needs that have no love in it. They are the souls that murder, inflict destruction, and never see the error of their ways. They are the ones that are oblivious to their surroundings and out of touch with their own soul and spirit. They are callous, but do not think they are. They only have a desire to be filled up with unreal selfish needs. These are the ones that may latch onto a human soul for the sake of coaxing them onto drinking, doing drugs or causing harm to another soul. They are the ones that cause pain in others on any level. Only this time the pain is mirrored back to them in the dark dimension.

    The dimension is like its namesake in that it is dark and dreary due to their manifestations. It is made up of false mirages that evaporate out of the sands when you draw near it. They are the lost souls relentlessly intending on shunning any form of light. Their confused soul craves a perpetual escape and freedom that is non-existing. They design situations that are toxic by feeding their soul rubbish. They are destined to be stuck in the dark dimension until they come to true consciousness. This is by stripping away the selfish tendencies, greed, self-destruction and excessive carnal pleasures. This is by exuding love in all directions. Only then can they truly move forward. This is a rare and difficult task as these are the same soul's that lived an Earthly life who refused such love when it was given. They do not change when they cross over. They resist the tunnel of light that would only free them of harsh circumstances and bathe them in love. When someone attempted to love them on Earth, they rejected that soul. They do the same in this dimension unable to be penetrated by the power of God's love. Know that the angels repeatedly attempt to bring the soul into the light and often succeed, but there are cases where it is difficult. Since all souls are granted free will choice, they cannot force a soul into the light, but merely guide them into the light.

God's love comes to human souls in many forms including the soul mates they encounter. When they enter a companionship with one soul in a love relationship, then this is the highest form of love lessons for them to experience. The love relationship is what teaches you to love and to compromise. It gives both souls companionship on their journey together. It is what is intended to teach you to give and receive equally in order to create balance. The love relationship teaches you to strip away your materialistic needs and grandiose narcissism when you allow it. It helps you remember what is important. It is the love of another human soul. Your soul benefits greatly from this form of relationship. The reason it benefits you more than any other is because you are joining forces with this person who is not like you. They might test you and bring out uncomfortable feelings that you must face in order to expand your consciousness. When you reject or ignore these connections that are divinely orchestrated, then you do not know love or God. This carefree nature is ego driven to satisfy what you want, which has no room for love or soul advancement. These are the souls that head towards the lifeless dimension as they cross over. They carry chains that hold them captive unable to break free of the padlocks of steel that formed from their materialistic and selfish desires. Learn about love while you are living an Earthly life now. Do not wait until your soul crosses over into the dimension that awaits you causing an even bigger delusion of who you are. Give love. Express love. Remember love. Do not treat others unkindly. Do not act out selfishly or recklessly with abandon. Remember who you are in truth and as a soul. Strip yourself of the toxic cravings you have that only weigh your soul down. Think of how you can serve humanity. You are not living an Earthly life to wallow in despair and pity or to chase greed or cause harm. You are here for the reasons of love which expand your consciousness. Take action steps to improve your soul today.

## Painting with God

God and my Spirit team have explained that manifesting is much like painting. He says that you envision what you want in your mind's eye. You hold the paintbrush in your hand. You gaze upon the canvas and paint your desires on this surface. There will always be parts of the canvas that have yet to be painted. It is this way because you are painting and erasing on the canvas depending on how you direct your thoughts. Your thoughts shift, vibrate and change throughout the day. When this happens you are painting over your previous image on the canvas, thus changing your reality in the process. You erase it and you paint something new. Sometimes you paint something bad and this is what you get. Sometimes you paint something good and then you back track. You think about what you want. When you do this you are picking up the paintbrush ready to paint this visual on your canvas, but then you take a few steps back. You stop yourself from painting the whole picture. You fear success and what might happen.

I asked, "Is this why bad people that do horrible things sometimes end up succeeding?"

God said, "That is correct, my child."

I felt my connection wavering. "Zadkiel connect me to God."

God replied, "I never left. You did."

"How do I stay with you?" I asked.

"You believe and it is done." He said.

He shows me an image of my soul on the other side as a Wise One and hunter. There is a bright light shining on vibrant flowers and the greenest grass. A radiant colored light shines out of my hands. Wherever I direct my hands, the light splashes images around me as if I am in my own painting. These images are the things my soul craves or desires. This is how you manifest. I asked God if this were possible.

He said, "You believe and then you doubt. This is how you disconnect from what you want. You forget who you are. You can create your reality. You do this where you came from before you took this current form. You did this effortlessly and never doubted. When you are home you will understand."

"Are you one person or soul?" I said, "Sometimes I have noticed that you refer to yourself as *we*."

"I am everywhere. I am in your Guides. I am in the Archangels. I am in the angels. I am in every planet, every cell, every tree, every mountain, every human, every cloud, every particle, every atom, every centimeter. I am in the best of your "self". I am in you. I am you."

"I get it." I said, "Can you tell me more about this painting concept?"

"I've shown you what you need to know."

"I was never painting the entire canvas. I would start to paint, but then erase some of it. I would erase the good. This is done by doubting."

"Now you understand." God said, "See the life you want and you shall have it. Never waver from this thought. If you negate that thought of what you want, if you are indecisive about it, then that is what you will get. Nothing. When you doubt you will get what you want for one second, then you forget who you are and therefore receive nothing. As you are a part of me, you have the power to paint what you want and receive it. There is no class you need to take. You are the example. You are the Light. You are a powerful manifester. Paint what you want on this canvas. Never sway from the good you desire. When you sway, you forget who you are and where you came from. Paint the entire canvas. Keep it painted everyday or it will evaporate off the page."

# Chapter Three

## MUSINGS ABOUT CONNECTING WITH THE SPIRIT WORLD

The next dimension, the spiritual plane that is right after this one, the place your soul travels to when you're done with this Earth class is closer than you think. Many believe it to be far, far, away and unreachable, if it even exists as some might say. It absolutely exists even if some Earthly souls are unable to fathom it. Some have lost hope or faith due to their life choices and circumstances. This causes them to express doubt. The next spiritual plane where most departed souls move to is three feet above the earth plane. This is why many gifted Mediums and Psychics successfully communicate messages from others in the spirit world so effortlessly. This is due to the spirit world being right above this plane running parallel three feet away. Keep in mind that the Earth plane is huge rising high above the clouds and into the ethers of what you know as "space" where the planets orbit. The first etheric plane above this one runs parallel above that. Actually "they" consider us and them as all one plane. I separate them to indicate that it is an entirely different world. There are other dimensions beyond the immediate etheric plane after this one where most souls move to next.

There are many gifted Mediums who communicate with the other side professionally. However, it is important to remember that you are also a gifted Medium whether you use your abilities or not. Like any muscle in your body, you need to work it and use it often. The more weights you lift at the gym with your body, the stronger your body becomes. The psychic muscle is the same concept.

When you have a psychic read, the future is always probable. What is seen coming up in your life can be altered significantly if you act on free will. For example, if you choose to deny the soul mate that is in your path repeatedly or you choose not to take a particular job, etc. This will alter your path and a new path is formed. For example, if you were meant to be in a long term soul mate relationship with someone, but the other person denied it and left, then they did so out of free will. Your spirit team will work with this soul mates team to bring you both together again. If this is unsuccessful, due to this person denying Heavenly guidance and acting out on free will, then your Spirit team will work to bring you a higher soul mate more aligned with you.

We all have varying ways of communicating with the other side. Some may be more open to seeing other souls that have departed, while others can feel them. You have those, such as myself, who hear them, as well as those who know they are present without questioning it. I have been hearing them for as long as I can remember. Some people use divination tools for confirmation of the messages they receive from the other side. Calling someone up with your telephone is similar to a divination tool. Spirit can deliver messages to you in a variety of ways, such as through your senses, through signs, symbols, and numbers or through the use of a divination tool such as an Angel Board, Tarot or Oracle deck. The tools are used to communicate or confirm what the reader is picking up on from the other side.

It can be painfully depressing to see some human souls unaware or confused and unsure of what is going on around them outside of the material world. Much of the hesitance some human souls have with crossing over is the fear of the light and that judgment or eternal Hell is associated with it. This is due to teachings during their upbringing on Earth. It is hammered into their psyches by those around them and adopted as second nature.

Your ego remains as is when you cross over. No longer stuck inside your human body, you carry the traits you had while living an Earthly life. This includes any negative traits or thought patterns. If you let go and move with the process of crossing over, you will notice any pain you were previously carrying being lifted off your soul effortlessly.

Those who pass onto the other side will at times visit their loved ones on Earth to make sure they are okay. Your departed loved ones are doing fantastic, but they know that you may not be or that you may not understand their death. My Spirit team has informed me that many of the departed souls tend to assist one or more of their grandchildren if they have any. Their own children are older than their grandchildren. Because they are older, they are likely set in their ways and do not need much guidance the way a younger person might.

It is okay if you do not know who to call when addressing an angel or guide. Simply calling out to Heaven will bring the right guide, angel or spirit who specializes in your specific case. You can request a Heavenly soul to assist you with something particular. Results are not always instant. You may have a soul on the other side working with you for several months. They will stay with you for however long it takes to fulfill what your request is. The spirit guide leaves when their assignment with you is complete. They move on to help other human souls requesting assistance. They often have their hands full when it comes to working with human souls, because they are dealing with souls who enjoy operating from ego or using free will, which can affect and alter their circumstances significantly.

When you struggle to receive Heavenly communication, then you block it from reaching you. The ethereal communication cord is much like a telephone wire to the other side. This dims considerably when there are blocks around you. Relax and let go of the need to receive a Heavenly message and allow it to flow into you naturally.

When you shift into a greater and more fulfilling spiritual life, you need to watch what you ingest into your body. You need to be mindful of what and whom you allow to hang around your vicinity. Your sensitivity is growing and can only absorb so much before it needs to recharge. It can no longer handle that much psychic input in one sitting. I had to make some strict lifestyle changes when my portal had cracked open again after having been bathed in addictions. There was a distinct difference in my connections when I was clear minded as opposed to being heavily intoxicated, high or after having consumed bad foods.

When you stop and detach from whatever emotional or stressful issue you are experiencing, then you are apt to receiving the answer needed from your Spirit team. When you are under stress or worry, then that blocks the communication lines with Heavenly helpers. Ask that your Spirit team remove and lift the stress and worry off your body so that you are more receptive to the answers and messages they are relaying to you.

Your first response as to who is communicating with you is the right answer. Second-guessing the information you receive pushes you further away from your initial hit of who or what it is. You will know who it is without a doubt in the world. Trust what you receive.

There is no greater feeling of freedom than connecting with Spirit. You can do this anywhere, but in a nature setting or calm atmosphere, will allow the connection to be clearer. This allows Spirit to lift the weight of your burdens off your soul. You realize that nothing else matters. Human egos force restrictions upon other human souls and have no basis in reality. The forces come from ones lower self and are typically born out of fear.

When guided, I often deliver messages I receive through Spirit to others, but then I walk away from it. All I do is act as the messenger in those cases. It is up to the person on the receiving end to decide how they wish to proceed or act with this information delivered. Never volunteer the information unless you are certain your Spirit team insists it will benefit someone in a positive way. Never divulge where you are getting the accurate messages from to a skeptic. When you are a messenger of God and Spirit, you must take great responsibility in the way you relay those messages.

All human souls have psychic abilities. "Psychic" is not reserved for the John Edwards' or Sylvia Browne's out there. Famous and well-known psychic mediums are where they are at because they have chosen to devote their lives to this work. They have turned it into a winning career. The same concept applies to how you are at your own job. When you have been with a company or doing a certain type of work for a long period of time, then you get better at it. You can almost do it blindfolded. This is essentially how successful psychics have turned what they do into a lucrative profession. No human soul is more special than anybody else. Everyone has diverse gifts with varying ranges within the realm of psychic abilities. It is all a matter of tuning in to discover what your specific gifts are and then re-developing that muscle. One works out their physical body this same way. You need to work your psychic muscle out as well. When you were born, your soul was 100% psychic, but you were also given the dreadful ego in order to test you. The ego creates roadblocks and barriers in all aspects of your life. You also learned negative behavior patterns from those around you. Those learned traits connect you to the material and superficial world. This is only some of a handful of things that can prevent someone from being in tune to spirit.

The ego is not a part of you to punish you, even though it seems to do a good job of it at times. Its intention is to challenge you. You must learn from your challenges. When you learn, then you grow. Growing your soul is in order to know what is right from wrong.

Since all human souls have egos this makes it difficult for the majority to believe or comprehend that they indeed are psychic. The word psychic has a negative connotation to it if one is a skeptic. They may not realize that they are picking up messages from their own Spirit Guide and Guardian Angel regularly. Everyone has at least one Spirit Guide and one Guardian Angel who is with them around the clock, from birth until death. They offer guidance along your path while answering some of your prayers on divine timing. If you are not listening or following this guidance, it can make your journey on Earth a bit bumpy.

You receive messages from beyond almost effortlessly when you are relaxed, stress free and happy. You also receive messages and guidance when you are tired. I have talked about how I successfully conducted a particular Mediumship session with a girl's departed loved one on the other side. I did this while running on no sleep. When you are in a fatigued state, then you are too tired to let your ego get in the way. It is fascinating that the human ego has incredible power that it can block someone from receiving messages from the other side.

A good place to start is by thinking back to particular circumstances where you might have professed something that later came true. You remember how that information came to you naturally from seemingly out of nowhere. Notice the way you came to this information and if it was the same process each time. This will give you a good direction on where your specific psychic abilities lie.

You are not alone and have at least one Guardian Angel and one Spirit Guide that works with you on the other side. Yet, you become absolved in your own neurosis and problems attempting to do it all on your own without accessing them. Many souls run into roadblocks or frustrations over something they are trying to make happen.

I have to stop them and say, "Have you asked for help?"

They will protest, "Oh you're right! I forgot about that."

I will get a message from them later. "I asked like you said and it worked! Wow!" They will describe the outcome of what happened after days of no movement. They asked for help and suddenly the answer they needed appeared.

You have to give your Spirit team permission to help you and intervene in your life. Let them know you want them to work with you. If you do not, they will sit their idly watching you wiggle around in stress and annoyance. Do not just ask them for help, but then let it go and let them get to work on it. When you let go, the resolution comes to you much more quickly.

There is one way you can tell the difference between heavenly guidance and your lower self or ego. When you receive messages from heavenly spirits, you will never experience fear, anxiety or dread. The messages they relay are full of love, even if they are warning you of something negative. There is still a sense of peace or an uplifting feeling that all is okay.

Sometimes I receive clairvoyant visions especially while experiencing a lucid dream sequence. This was the case where my Spirit team delivered a message to me when I was in a deep sleep. In this instance, they were showing me what many around the world were going through at that particular time. In the dream, they are taking me into what might appear to be a nightmare to the average person. I can handle most anything and I am used to some of the abrupt ways delivered messages reach me.

I walked into my house and a man was standing there. Naturally, as you might do, I wondered why he was in my house. He approached me and asked me for money. Without thinking twice I said, "Sure." I reached into my pocket, but then he quickly moved towards me in an uncomfortable way. I asked, "What are you doing?" Before anything else could happen, he pulled out a blade and stabbed me in the heart with force. I felt a huge sharp pain as if it was really happening and I was dying. The piercing of the stab in my heart was pulling me deeper into the other world. My eyes shot open and I realized it was no longer happening. I collected myself and then brushed it off knowing it was a divine message. I knew they would reveal additional information to the stabbing image when I would fall back asleep again for part two.

I fell into another deep sleep not long afterwards to allow my Spirit team to give me the rest of the message. I heard a loud banging like construction echo going on for minutes before it stopped. I wandered through the house in the dark at 3:00 am. I was wide-awake and noticed the tiling from some of the walls were broken and crumbled all over the floor. I could see the pipes within the walls. I saw pieces of the plaster on the floor in other rooms too. I glazed over it confused and perplexed. Mind you, it was happening as if it were real time. There was no comprehension that it was a dream. My eyes shot open and I looked around noticing everything was fine. No tiling or plaster on the floor. I knew then that it never happened.

I did not have to ask my team for more clarification because I understood their language and message. They filtered the messages through my crown chakra. The stabbing in my heart was telling me that it was to deliver the message that many around the world are experiencing heartbreaks in breakups of all kinds. This was backed up by the abundant amount of messages from readers I was receiving. They were all experiencing a hard relationship break up at the same time. The deterioration and crumbling of the walls in my home in the darkness were telling me that these breakups were significantly painful and happening out of nowhere. The darkness is the heavy grieving felt. Those who were experiencing these break ups and endings were feeling as if their whole world was crumbling down. The structure and stability they had come to understand was falling apart. There was much heartbreak within the dynamic of many of the connections. This was no surprise to me because at the time we were in the midst of the Venus Retrograde transit. This causes relationships of all kinds to break apart abruptly or the connections are strained.

When you experience the kind of heartbreak where you cannot find the will to pull yourself back up, call on heavenly assistance. Archangel Raphael can help bring feelings of peace and serenity. Archangel Azrael can help make the pain and transition out of a bad relationship much easier than without heavenly assistance. Archangel Raquel can help restore balance within you and your partner, friend, or whoever you experienced an abrupt issue or ending with. Know that you are not alone or ignored. It may not seem like it when you are going through heartbreak, but it is happening for a reason that will become apparent at the right time.

The Archangels are powerful, benevolent beings who can show up for anyone who asks. They are unlimited after all. Archangel Michael is with me on a daily basis and always shows up even when I do not specifically request him. This is because I made a pact with him a long time ago that he would be my protector on my journey here. In another incident, I was in a deep sleep and within another vivid dream as if it was happening in real time. There was a nasty dark ugly poltergeist throwing things at me and around me. Poltergeist or noisy ghosts exist. They are not as bad as Hollywood horror films like to portray. These spirits do not realize what they are doing. They are stuck in a limbo atmosphere, which is similar to the Earth plane, but no place for any roaming soul. This poltergeist in the dream was intense due to its real nature and by infiltrating itself into my dream. My heart fell into my stomach and I ran out of breathe. I shouted in the dream, "Archangel Michael!" A huge boom sound rang out loudly like a native drum. My surroundings lit up with super bright light. My eyes shot open as I caught my breath. An overwhelming feeling of love took over my soul.

Some have lucid or vivid dreams which evaporate upon wakening. Sometimes this is due to the use of drugs and alcohol. The effects of drugs and alcohol interrupt ones sleep cycle and diminish the amount of REM (dream state) input. This can cause you to forget your dreams upon waking. When you release the need to consume drugs and alcohol, your body will go through an automatic detox. The detox process is not always smooth as inner stuff is coming out of you. When you are no longer on negative substances, your dreams become more lucid. Your consciousness travels out of your body during your dream state. Often times when going through withdrawals or detoxing, even months after the elimination, can lead you to experience fear in your dreams. Your subconscious mind and your lower self are in a tug of war while in the sleep state.

Use of alcohol and drugs hinder the brain chemicals that transmit messages. When you no longer consume heavy amounts of negative substances, then your brain's neurotransmitters go through a process of re-alignment. Part of this causes an out of body experience. Some will experience flying dreams as well as dream situations surrounding fear. Your soul is not grounded in the physical world. This can assist you in delving deeper into working with methodologies of healing and working with your clairvoyance. Remembering your dreams and having repetitive out of body experiences are signs that your third eye and clairvoyance have opened or are in the process of opening.

As a sensitive vibrational being, you will sense things more than the average person would. You enter a store where everyone else seems okay with the energy, yet your Spirit team gives you a warning sign to leave the store. You feel it in your gut area and perhaps your heart rate accelerates. You might hear your Spirit team calmly ask you to leave the store. They ask you to purchase your items somewhere else. Some of these warnings might happen while in a metaphysical store as a reader named Karen explained to me. She believed that because psychics practice there that it must be okay. Unfortunately, that is not always the case. Someone within the store may operate heavily on ego or they are unable to reel the ego in. This can attract in negativity into these stores. Perhaps a hostile client wandered into the store that day and their energy was so intense that it stayed in the store long after they left. You will know if it's not safe if you walk into the store and suddenly you experience negative thoughts or mood.

Everyone has the ability to connect and communicate with a spirit guide or angel. Some see it, others hear it, some feel it, while others know it. Pay attention to your senses as they are communication channels with the other side.

Have it set in your mind that they communicate with you every day. The more you practice, remain aware and in tune to your senses, the easier it gets to work with them. You are always communicating with them, even if you may not realize the messages you are picking up on are indeed your Spirit team.

Sometimes someone might experience a specific health scare or near death condition that re-opens the portal to Spirit. Those situations crack it open for good. I talk about how this process happened for me in my book, *"Reaching for the Warrior Within"*. My connections have been ongoing since I was coherent, but there was a health scare in particular that cracked it wide open again. It was the turning point for me as I shifted into a higher consciousness. There was no going back to my previous life and I would not have had it any other way. Archangel Michael visibly appeared as the introduction to what the next chapter and beyond would be.

It is not always up to the angels or Heaven to do it all for you. It is up to you. When will you take action? When you take action, then Heaven meets you more than half way. They will not hand anything to a human soul who sits around doing nothing, but waiting and complaining on when life will hand them something great. Heaven waits patiently for this soul to see the blessings they have around them. They watch this soul put in the work required before they intervene.

# Chapter Four

## LAW OF ATTRACTION

Successful people have at least one thing in common. They are optimistic when it comes to what they want to achieve. They fixate on their desire with unwavering strength and focus. Heaven does not want you to suffer, but your ego will do whatever it takes to ensure you experience downfall. Heaven and your team of Guides and Angels understand that you have basic human needs. When you are happy and fulfilled in all areas of your life, your Spirit team knows that you are more apt to focusing on your life's purpose. The daily choices you make can block the flow of abundance without you realizing it. Sometimes it can be a perpetual cycle of negative thoughts that run through your mind. Perhaps you sit in traffic every day to and from work with anger or stress. This negative mindset constructs a block on your road to abundance. Your words and thoughts have a powerful energy vibration. It effortlessly brings you something of equal value. If your words and thoughts are mostly negative, then this is what you're going to bring to you. You either bring in more negative circumstances to you, or you bring in nothing. These are the human souls that complain that it feels as if they've been stagnant forever with little to no movement. If you spend your entire day doing nothing or partaking in time wasting activities of a low vibration, then you have made a choice. All of your choices have a cause and effect in what is to come to you. Take note when you made a decision in your past that potentially altered your intended course. You may be able to recall how this choice caused a preferred or undesired effect. The goal is to be aware of your thoughts, words and the choices you make throughout your day. This is how to stop yourself from making a decision that you know will set off an entire array of unwanted results. When you connect and tune in with your own higher self, then you become fully conscious of the choices you make. If you make a decision that you know deep down is going to cause unhappiness to yourself or someone else, then re-consider your approach. Notice how unnecessary the choice might be when compared to the ultimate outcome. Your lower self and ego makes choices in haste, or in an impulsive burst of suffocating energy. It is bathed in overwhelming negative emotion and then this is what you bring more of to you.

Allow any damaging baggage in your life to fade away. Carefully plan the next few years of your life. When deep in thought or meditation, focus in on what it is you dream of or desire. For example, say a positive affirmation such as, "I'm going to buy a home that will be the foundation of my life." Ask your Spirit team for help with this. Tell them what you want and give them an area, "I will buy an affordable Condo in this area and here's how much money I have." Sit down with your Spirit team and visualize what you want with them. Envision exactly how you want your life to be in a year. Before you know it, it will be the end of the year and it will be exactly that. Human souls need steady, stability and calm. This state of mind is the perfect breeding ground to raise your vibration and attract in positive abundance. Love yourself and all the good that you have within you, because you are awesome!

## Visualizing Your Reality

Visualize how you want your life to be. Even if it seems impossible, do it anyway. Feel it in your gut and in every cell of your body. Believe it as if it is already happening. This can be from the career you want, relationship, home, or anything you desire pending it is not harmful to you or someone else. Aligning it with your higher self's purpose is the way to create good Karma. Visualizing circumstances that are harmful to you or someone else is dangerous. It will backfire and become part of your Karmic thread, even if it is initially a success. Eventually it is a debt that has incurred on your soul that must be paid back. When someone's ego wants something with great veracity, then it is not in a high vibrational state of mind to understand the consequences until it's too late. Never discredit the power of your mind. You have the power to create your reality. You are creating your reality whether you're fully aware of this or not. You can have anything you want as long as you hold the intention with positive thoughts. Allow your mind to wander into a daydream visualizing the life you want. Remember that if a thought has any doubt in it, then this can negate or delay what you want from happening. Therefore it is important to catch yourself when distrust creeps into your mind. When this happens and you are aware of it, then mentally say, "Cancel that thought and replace it with this." Modify the negative thought with something positive in exchange. Some of history's immense talents, leaders and CEO's are in the positions they're in because they do not allow insecurity or negative self-talk to stop them from accomplishing what they intend to. They set intentions without negative interference. They know exactly what they want with unwavering excitement surrounding this desire. They go after it with enormous gusto and they get it! If you witness successful leaders in action, you will find they are precise, focused and optimistic.

# THOUGHTS PRODUCE CIRCUMSTANCES

Negative thoughts cause the majority of human unhappiness. It is true that challenges happen for a reason. If you do not have challenges, then you do not learn, grow and overcome. When you are aware of the challenges, then you are able to shift them into something positive. Being aware of them is to have an understanding of why a challenge took place. Avoid losing sight of what is important on your journey here. It is easy to veer off track when functioning in this material based world on a regular basis. Take a little bit of time out daily to detach from the chaos around you. This is to avoid permanently drowning in the ego based noise of the world. Days pass by and you discover you are going through the motions. Your thoughts move into words of a lower vibration, thus bringing more of this to you.

You are always creating your own future reality. When bathed in negative thoughts, it will soon make it seem as if nothing is going your way. Suddenly you receive a parking ticket, or you get into a car accident, or you are pulled over. Next thing you know you are running into one person after another who is making you feel even more miserable. It turns into a domino effect that continues forward without any hope of escape. You become immersed in it to the point where you're oblivious to the fact that you created this reality. This consistent negative reality persists for weeks. You complain about it with anyone who will listen from friends, family, to colleagues. This lowers their vibration in the process. Those around you soak up this energy since it latches onto their aura. They begin to exude this same behavior and spread it around to others as well. You can see how this can get out of hand. A movement of this negative outbreak infects the entire planet. For some, this carries on for years and even decades! They do not believe they are the cause of this and therefore are unaware that they have the power to stop this cycle. This is why no one can deny the planet is in complete chaotic angry disarray. Turn on the media or visit a social networking site. Most of it contains a diatribe of complaints.

The words are easy to detect because they can be negative, judgmental, critical and abusive towards yourself or others. The reason that we use the word vibration or energy is because they are invisible particles in the air that many might not be accustomed to understand. Human ego believes something to be non-existent if it is unseen. You have more power than you realize. You have the power to manipulate this energy in your surroundings and bring forth to you that which you desire. Keep your thoughts and words high vibrational in order to attract in abundance.

If you find you're buried in negativity, then it is time for a soul time out. Escape from the noise around you and retreat to somewhere quiet. Close your eyes for a moment and relax. Take a deep breath in and exhale. Change the negative sentences, complaints, or worries which your mind is repeatedly stating. Shift them into something positive. You can do this by starting your sentences with, "I love…"

"I love myself. I love who I am. I love that I have a car that runs. I love that I have a job that pays all my bills." And so forth.

Practice shifting your words to those of gratitude. If you find you're moving back into negativity and destructive thoughts, then be conscious of this and shift it once again. Re-word your sentences to more positive uplifting ones. It is work re-training your mind to get to that place, but with practice and over time, you will get better at it. The results will be astounding when you find that great things begin coming your way. You discover that your life has become less stressful. Negativity is a learned trait. Most of it stems from childhood conditioning. You unknowingly adopt it as second nature. This is why breaking those bad habits down or diminishing them can take some time and work on your part to bring your soul to the high vibrational space it was when you were first born.

The Archangel Michael vacuums away all dark energy. Visualize him holding an ethereal vacuum hose. He takes this hose and inserts it into your crown chakra above your head and down into your body. Imagine that he turns the vacuum on and sucks out any negative, dirty ion debris lodged within and around your body. Some of this negativity hardens if you've been harboring it for some time. Allow him to remove all traces of this toxic negativity within and around your body and soul leaving you feeling uplifted and optimistic. Let go of all burdens and concerns and hand it over to him for transmutation. Once you release the need to control the outcome of your worries, the more likely it will resolve itself in a rapid fashion. If you have been hanging onto tons of negativity, then do this clearing daily until you know or sense that it is gone. At that point, you will be much better at managing it and extricating it from your vicinity when it happens again. It is advised to do a routine cleaning once in awhile if you live in a heavily populated area, since this is where negative energy expands on a daily basis.

## DAYDREAM

Avoid getting caught up in the noise and drama of the world's nasty behavior. Human drama flies out from all angles on a regular basis. It is erratic and unstable. It does nothing to help you or anybody. Take regular time outs than necessary, and relax and smile more. Shun going to places where you know it is going to be taxing on your system. Go for walks alone *(or with a love interest)* and daydream. Do this in a nature setting if possible. Daydream about beautiful, wonderful circumstances and feelings. Think about the amazing blessings you currently have, and then daydream about what you would like to see manifest next in your life. If your life is where you want it, then daydream about that more. Take walks in areas where you know it will not be crowded with people. I've witnessed others attempting to go for a stroll in busy cities only to dodge restless and reckless drivers nearly running them over. You're on guard and your heart rate shoots up on high alert every time you have to cross a busy street with impatient drivers. This is no way to relax and center your soul. Venture off into a nature setting whenever possible for strong effectiveness. Find a quiet place to focus or meditate on anything that is not man-made. This can be something like a sunset, a plant, flower, or mountain peak.

The moon phases and cycles have a larger energy power behind them. Check online or a planetary calendar for the dates of the New Moon and Full Moon phases. Most calendars tend to have those two transits listed for each month. The New and Full Moon transits add extra manifesting energy to your thoughts. Be careful with your thoughts more than usual during those moon phases. Keep them positive and upbeat. If your mind goes into worry or something negative, you are going to bring about more of that to you! The New Moon is a great time to start a new positive activity or regimen. This can be beginning a new relationship, job or even sending out your resume. The New Moon symbolizes new beginnings. The Full Moon has immense manifestation power as well. The Full Moon is typically a nice phase to release bad habits or people, while aligning your focus with what you truly desire.

Do whatever it takes to get you to that place of feeling happy and content. This can be anything small from watching a funny, uplifting movie, to hanging out with a cheerful friend who always makes you laugh. Place your work and worries aside and celebrate your life. Be grateful for what you currently have. See your soul and where you're at in a positive light. See the blessings that you have in your life right now. Do not think about or worry over what is coming next or what is not here. Put that all aside and let loose and enjoy yourself. Learn to celebrate this life and insist on having more good times.

It is inevitable that you will hit a rough patch in your

Earthly life. This might be where your soul feels lost, overly emotional, or lethargic. Sometimes these feelings signify that you are on the precipice of grand changes needing to happen in your life. It is a transformative period prompting you to be more introspective. What matters is how you work through the issues that this energy is bringing out of you. What it creates within you might be uncomfortable as it is asking you to examine where you are at in your life. This can be in any area such as career, relationships or health.

Learn from your current circumstances, choices and experiences. Avoid remaining mired in negative feelings and thoughts. Heavy emotions force you to be hyper-focused on where you are at. This prompts you to feel stuck as if you are trapped in an eternal prison. Yucky feelings stall your progress and forward movement. It becomes difficult to reach a place of happiness while in that state. In order to work through these feelings and thoughts, you have to examine them with a fine toothcomb. Look for the underlying cause and message that continues to prompt you to obsess over thoughts which have no basis in reality. What areas in your life are provoking you in a negative way? Those are areas which require a necessary change. Ask your Spirit team for assistance and follow their guidance, even if they push you out of your element. Know they do this for your own higher self's good. It is a sign that it is a time to move on to the next plateau. See only the love and lessons in the experiences you are asked to modify or leave. Make your peace with it in order to move to a brighter, content life.

## Money, Success, Abundance

Everyone deserves to live comfortably without worry. Even if you're twenty years old, create supplemental and retirement income today. Before you know it, you will be forty years old and wonder why you had not started earlier.

When you take one action step at a time towards your goal, you will be that much closer to seeing your dream happen. One of the positives of the modern day world we live in is that everything is at your disposal. It is not like earlier history, or the 20$^{th}$ Century, where everyone had to rely on corporate greed to have the opportunities to express their talents. Those days are no more and thank God. You are able to go out there and put it together yourself at any age. The plusses of the digital world are that it allows one to successfully work for themselves.

All human souls want to live comfortably happy. This is in knowing that your bills are paid on time without any struggle while having more time to pursue personal luxuries and focus on your purpose here. Sometimes it might feel like you are taking a step forward and then a step back. This is much like the image of a spiral staircase. You are not going backwards or having a setback. Rather you are going around and then up.

When you focus your sole attention on obtaining money, then you shut off the supply. Do not believe that money is your security. Look to God as your source of security. This is how abundant manifestation flows freely. You work for, "God, Incorporated." When you need supplies, then you ask for it. It is only when you say the words with intent that it soon takes form. Success is not always financial. It can be a state of mind where you feel grateful and are optimistic with what you have, where you are at and how far you have come. It is to take note of the great progress you have made to date.

Understand that money is only paper. Back around the B.C. ages, humankind created money by using things like sticks and stones. This was in order to obtain certain living essentials. We were not paying for these necessities, but rather exchanging it for goods. There is an exchange of energy. You're giving something to receive something. Soon the sticks and stones were manufactured into paper with dollar amounts and symbols on it. Human ego placed great emphasis and need on this paper. This pushed it further away from them. The real moneymaker is your higher self, the YOU of all you, God, the source, whatever you want to call it. Your thinking and limited reasoning mind is not. Let that all go and focus on the source for your abundance. Say affirmations such as: *"All of my needs and supplies are met in every way and in all directions of time."*

## MANIFESTING

The key to manifesting is having an unwavering passion for a desire. You can have anything you want and can cause anything to happen when you have unbending passion for it. This is where you feel this passion for your desire all over you, within you, and around you. You feel and know it in your mind. You feel and know it in your heart. You feel and know it all throughout your body and soul. You know without a doubt that it will happen and that it is here now. It's allowing this feeling to build to the intensity of an erupting volcano. You feel this desire continue to rise with positive excitement from within. There are no negative feelings associated with this passionate feeling. You visually see what you want happening in reality with great optimism. If you are having a passion for obtaining something, but you have doubts circling that, then the doubts will overpower the desire and you will receive the doubts instead of the desire. Experience inner peace and uplifting joy that you're living this vision as if it is real time. It is seeing this vision as if it is here and happening now. Hold this intention everyday and avoid negative thoughts from taking over. It is not enough to visualize something you want, but to also take action steps to get there. When you have a passion for something, you naturally want to dive into that passion. Having passion is a joyous feeling. It's the key to manifesting positively.

Once this is complete, the most difficult step is to then let it go. It's to release this vision and desire of what you want to your higher self, God, or your Spirit team. It's completely letting go of this desire and not caring about it. It's releasing and surrendering it to a higher power. The reason this is a challenging step is because most people find it difficult to let go of something they really want. They fixate on it heavily never letting the desire go. This then moves into obsessive doubts and concerns that it will never happen. However, if this last step is not followed, and you do not let this desire go and release it, then the manifestation connection is not fully made. It may push the outcome further away from you. This gives you an idea as to why your desire is not coming to fruition. You must let it go and move onto the next manifestation. Do not concern yourself with the how or when a manifestation will occur as this will block it. If you obsess over a desire, then you will block it from manifesting. Instead, you will receive negative manifestations or you'll find that you're in a stagnant position where there is no movement at all.

I've always been manifesting, as everyone is manifesting whether they're aware of it or not. I've been manifesting since I was a teenager through this process I describe. When I was sixteen, I knew I would be an author, but I also knew I would have to obtain a regular job first. I needed a steady income. If I were attempting to work on my dream as an author while worrying about not having a paycheck, then this would block me from achieving this dream. My Spirit team revealed the film business to me. They let me know that I would get a job in the creative side of the business, where I'd incorporate my love for storytelling and writing. I knew I was going to get into the entertainment business and nothing was going to stop me. When I was sixteen years old my mantra was: "I'll keep trying to get in until I'm 80." I studied books about the business and then went after notable production companies at full force. I got in the door right after my 23rd birthday. This was when I started working for one of the top ten most bankable and popular actresses at that time. Not surprisingly one of my main roles for her was to read scripts and provide written coverage or a synopsis on the work. I graduated from that particular class, after she dissolved her production company. I then made a move into coordinating film production shoots for the major studios. This was followed by me making the transition into work as an author. This is the quick cliff note version, but hammers home that I knew what I wanted with a burning desire, I went after it and got it.

Many struggling to get into Hollywood have always asked me what my secret was to getting in. I was passionate about it. I knew I was going to get into the industry. I had a steady, calm, euphoric positive energy surrounding what I wanted. I use the word passion to describe this process. If you don't have passion for something, then it will show. It doesn't matter what your expertise is or what kind of degree you have. None of that matters. If you have no passion and it shows, then you can forget about attracting your desire in. You need to passionately want it, but then let go of knowing, how or when it will happen.

When I first started out in the entertainment business, I had no skills or experience to warrant getting a job in that industry. All I had to sell them was my personality, drive and passion. I walked in there and conveyed how much I wanted it and how right I was for the gig. There was no acting needed, because I genuinely wanted it with incredible veracity. I went after every job position with this same passion and I was hired. This same manifestation process was the same process for how I became an author. I knew I was going to do it. I clairvoyantly saw it up ahead. I've been following my own Spirit team's guidance, messages, and steps relayed to me from as far back as a teenager. This same process was also the case with all of the relationships I was involved in. I knew without a doubt that I would be with a particular person. Granted, I'm sure in hindsight, I might have paid bigger attention to the red flags presented, but the point is to be careful what you wish for. If the wish is felt with great positive veracity, passion, and steadfast intensity, then you will get it!

# Chapter Five

## Transform Your Work Life

One of the biggest complaints and grumblings I hear others protest about is how tired they always are. Feeling tired even when you are getting an average of eight hours of sleep a night can partially be a symptom of depression. You might not even realize you are depressed because you equate the 'depression' word to be associated with feeling down or someone prone to crying in despair. This is not true. Many work at jobs they hate or are unhappy at, while others are unemployed for a great deal of time. Some work at jobs that pay just enough to survive. Weeks, months and then years of this pass and the weight of these effects start to take its toll on you. Terribly unhappy with poor diets and lifestyle choices coax you onto reaching for bad foods and addictions in hopes of instantaneous comfort. The opposite is ego driven exercising, which is a form of addiction. This is when one merely works out to look desirable to others. When one is unhappy with their work life, it pushes them to reach for an addiction to keep going. Being unhappy in a relationship is significantly different. Those who are unhappy in a relationship will dive more into work or they leave their mate. When someone is unhappy at work, but their relationship is fine, they rarely dive into their relationship. For one, most people unhappy at work are working 40 hours a week, which is more time spent than anywhere else. The irony is that those who are unhappy find it easier to walk away from their love relationships in an impulse, but will stay at an unhappy job for years simply because it's paying the bills. You allow your job to rule you. Your job is paying your bills, but in the end when your soul crosses over, it becomes obsolete. What matters are the relationships you had with others that have more of a profound impact on your soul in the end. Your relationships are worth saving over an unhappy job.

More people resort to some form of anti-depressant or anti-anxiety medication than ever before. While there is nothing wrong with any form of medical treatment, you do want to make sure you are not on medication for the sole reason of shutting life out permanently. On the flip side, those who might be against anti-depression medication may be the ones who are abusing an unhealthy addiction to *numb the pain*. This would come in the guises of food, drugs, cigarettes or alcohol. No one around me knows more about numbing the pain than I do. I used to consume anything and everything that was bad for me in order to feel bliss if even temporarily. Often it was on purpose just to cause my soul harm. As much as there are benefits to taking anti-depressants for those who absolutely need them, the down side is that is what contributes to a zombie like emotion-less state of mind. I am not advocating that you stay away from anti-depressants, because they do help a great deal of people who absolutely need them. Life has been tough for so many that they may be unable to pull through. Anti-depressants under the care of a physician can help restore and re-train your mind. The challenge is when you wane off the medication and attempt to forge on in life anti-depressant free. I was on anxiety medication for several years at one point in my life. They did help me get through two relationship break-ups with those who were emotionally unavailable. Those connections coaxed me to take back control of my life and not rely on someone else for my emotional comfort. It also prompted me to discover what I do not want in a love relationship. I would not accept anything less than stability, compassion, love, and trust in a romantic potential.

The average person works full time. This means they are working 40 hours a week, which is roughly 160 hours or so a month. A large chunk of your time is spent at a job every day with no end in sight. Ensure that you are participating in meaningful work that makes you happy. Couple that with you working with people that you have a positive synastry with. If one or either of those things is not in place, then you will fall into a stress-filled depression. Those unhappy at their job are afraid to leave. They fear dusting off their resume's, getting back out there and taking a chance in a new work place. They have bills to pay and they find some comfort in the security that the job they are at provides.

Perhaps your job is paying the bills and you appreciate that, yet you are still terribly unhappy inside. You are unfulfilled in your life. You're working at a job that you do not enjoy. You find you have to convince yourself to love it just to get through the day. There are several factors, which cause you to feel despondent. One of them can be that you hate the work you do. Perhaps you are stuck in a cubicle and would prefer to be working somewhere in the outdoors in nature. What is a redeeming feature is that you enjoy the people you work with and love the company. You have just enough to keep going, but is it enough?

What if you not only despise the work you are doing, but you also experience discomfort about one or more of the people you work with. You can be working with one person who you find antagonistic or pessimistic. They are toxic and negative in numerous ways. They can be abusive, which is the worst kind of person to be around. Not all abusive people are aware that they are this way. They are unhappy about where their life is too. This spills over to the rest of the staff. Then there is the narcissistic abusive colleague or boss. They are the ones that are aware they're abusive and yet they do not care. They believe that instilling fear is how to be powerful and exert their dominance. Exerting ones dominance through aggressive behavior comes from fear, which has zero power. This is the same trait that a bully has. It overcompensates in an attempt to cover up the real weakness they hide. Assertive and compassionate people have the highest vibrational power. They come off diplomatic and strong while winning respect and a team player attitude from others in the process.

You despise going into work and do not look forward to it, and yet you do it anyway. You do it because you are responsible and you have personal responsibilities to take care of, but inside you wonder if the horrid cycle will ever end. This downtrodden aura around you shows when you are at work, and then you bring it home to infect others you live with. You're the one the others in the office consider to be the unhappy camper. People who feel joy and contentment will shine and radiate. They are self-assured and lovable while still running an ordered ship. Find work that you love and avoid selling yourself out for a paycheck. Spending years at a job you despise will crush your spirit. This is heartbreaking and will keep your soul feeling trapped. Perhaps you work 160 hours a month at a job you despise, and on top of that you work with someone toxic. It is one thing if it is a colleague, but if it is your boss, then that adds an additional amount of issues weighing your soul down. Working at an unhappy job lowers your vibration and keeps it there until you break away from it. Breaking away from it can be through force, such as the company lays you off or fires you. You finally leave the company, or your soul gives out and you leave the Earth plane to head back home to Heaven.

Every morning the world sits in traffic attempting to race to work. You cannot race to work when you have endless cars in front of you moving at various speeds. For the most part, they are all riding with each other, but then you have the one person who is driving too slow or too fast. Everyone is a heart attack waiting to happen for many reasons. It is not just the obscene traffic. It must be stated since this is a common complaint among the 9-6 working class. They are either too tired from not enough sleep or they are fueled up on an abundant amount of caffeine and sugar. All of these exasperates and confuses your state of mind. When you are too tired, then you function in a haze. Your judgment is off and so are your thoughts and emotions. Pumping yourself up on high amounts of caffeine and sugar raises your blood pressure and causes hypertension, not to mention high levels of anxiety. You react erratically to every tiny little thing. This causes more unhappiness and blocks the communication lines from Heaven. The communication lines to Heaven are where the answers are to pull you out of this human designed trap.

    The majority of people work in jobs they hate, or work with antagonistic and toxic people. You deal with at least one personality that never jives with your own. This is what your life has become. This is what dominates your world since your job is where you're physically at most of the week. It is difficult to shake it off. You know you fall into this bracket when you leave work at the end of the day and you're too tired to do anything. Instead you head straight home to collapse while shielding yourself off from the noise of the world. If you are not going home, you are heading to the bar with colleagues or friends to decompress, vent or complain while drinking alcohol. Even the media perpetuates this ritual in entertainment where friends head to drink together at the bar to find bliss. This temporarily masks the issues and unhappiness. It does not permanently remove it. The next day the hole that has become your life is in plain view in front of you. If you are not meeting up with friends or colleagues for drinks after work, you are drinking at home to take the edge off. If you are in a relationship, you might take it out on your mate. However, if you are in a healthy love relationship, you may talk it over calmly. Couples in healthy relationships know about balancing the good with the bad. You retreat to each other feeling safe from the noise. Long term healthy love relationships raise your vibration just by being in each other's company and presence. Unfortunately, in this modern day progressive world, many complain they also find it difficult to find a long term loving relationship to begin with. Loyalty and commitment are lacking more than ever in history. This is what happens when your ego rules the roost. It wants to do what it wants you to do without any consequence or regard for others.

The ones that have it down are those who live in areas where there is a low population of people, living in or close to nature, and/or who work for themselves, and/or are in healthy long term love relationships. If you've got all of these, then you're likely in that space of beautiful contentment. There are those that love their job in the big city, but you do not love your job if whenever it is a workday you stress over the slightest disruption. It shows when you love your job. You are the one who is the calm within the storm. You are peaceful, centered and happy. All of these traits radiate around this person on a regular basis.

Tyler found that working a 9-6 job for someone else doing menial tasks only bored him. It was depressing and crushed his spirit little by little until he was permanently dejected. He would pump himself up with caffeine all day long. He did not drink soda or coffee, but he would use sports powders and B vitamin-energy powders so that he was at least getting some amino acids and vitamins. Although this is slightly better than soda, there are still other chemicals in there that should not be. They contributed to boosting his energy levels in some unnatural way. He would do this to pump himself up with excitement in order to gather enough energy to pretend to be into his job and get through the day. By the time the day was over, he would crash and collapse at home before he tranquilized himself to sleep at night. He would repeat this mantra the next day and so forth. Can you imagine the brevity of this behavior over the long-term?

The self-made prison he created was for a paycheck. He

was grateful that he had a paycheck, but this Monday thru Friday ten hours a day drained him. He would wake up at around 7:00 every morning, fight traffic for a half an hour when it should be fifteen minutes. By the time he was back home and settled in, it was 7:00 at night. Sometimes it was eight at night or beyond if he made a stop at the gym or the store. He did not always feel like jumping in the shower to head out with friends. There was zero motivation for much else. He would have an hour or so left to eat and relax before he needed to wind down to get to bed at a decent hour. This is a minimum 8-hour sleep cycle requirement that everyone should aim for. Imagine how tired Tyler would be if he also had chosen to start a family with children. He would likely have to nix the strict 8 hour sleep schedule.

If you find that you are sleeping at least eight hours a night, and yet you are still tired, then you might have adrenal fatigue. This is that no matter how much sleep you get, you are still tired throughout the day. To get through each day, you stuff yourself with caffeine in any source you can get. This only masks an even bigger problem that includes you not being as happy as you think you are in your life. When you are happy, then you experience a natural uplifting high. It is an alert energy you access from God or Higher Power. You crave very little caffeine if any. The stresses of each day are hard on your system and this causes this type of fatigue. The depression symptoms are still there, because unhappy people have some measure of depression. Check with your doctor to make sure there are no potential issues within you beyond feeling tired and depressed around the clock. If you check out fine, then depression and adrenal fatigue may be the common ailment causing this low energy within you. Either way your doctor can adequately diagnose you. It is equally important to examine the trouble areas in your life that could be the underlying cause. When you ask for heavenly assistance, your Spirit team can guide you to the remedies that are beneficial for your case.

Americans specifically and some other parts of the world

have this work and no play attitude. They have created a five-day work week when it should really be a four-day work week. Most people who work this type of schedule are not productive on Friday's. Some companies release their employee's mid-day on Friday. Many European countries do not observe the work them into the ground mentality. They have the four-day work week utilized. It is second nature to human souls to work five-day work weeks like dogs. This was programmed by the human ego.

Do you want to go out Friday night? Forget it. Many professionals have little to no energy for that unless it is work related and they have to. By the time the weekend rolls around, most of the working force spends Saturday running around playing catch up on practical matters. Sunday you cannot do much either since it is truly your only real day off. If you have families, then you know the demands of that time as well. Children see their parent or parents moping around the house exhausted and moody. When the uneventful weekend ends quickly, you dive right back into the unhappy work week angry and bitter. Years of this scenario pass by. You reminisce about what you wish your life could be like, and yet you never take any steps to get there.

Tyler wanted to have a career where he runs the show. He wanted successful self-employment, but he allowed negative thoughts to pervade him by asking questions like, "How many people actually get to do that?" As long as you have passion for it, then you can most certainly have that. Keep the faith and build your side business while working at your job. Remain optimistic and positive that the abundance will come in over time. When that happens, then you will be able to quit your day job and focus on your passion full time. You will be able to buy that house you have always wanted with an all cash offer. Home paid for and done!

Your future is changeable and psychically forecasted as probable. Due to your daily choices and actions, you might unknowingly alter your course with a decision or non-decision. You are the manager of your life. You are responsible for the choices you make. This is not saying that just because you find yourself in one toxic scenario after another that you are asking for it. It is a wake-up call to stop the cycle. The way to do that is to make different choices in your life. Break the pattern and make decisions that you might not normally make, or ones that might not be popular. Watch your life start to shift in a new, brighter way. Have faith that change is not only on the horizon, but that it is happening now. Accept that you will no longer be a victim of your circumstances.

If you are at an unhappy job, then start taking steps to change that. Schedule at least one day a week to explore your options for a new job. If you want to turn your hobby into a career, then start putting in some effort into it at least thirty minutes to an hour each day. Taking these steps and having a disciplined routine will start to raise your vibration and help you in attracting in the right kind of work for your temperament.

Ask your Spirit team on the other side for help. Tell them what you want and give them permission to intervene. You can say something like: *"Please help me find a great job that is aligned with my purpose. This is one that ensures all of my bills are paid. And so it is. Thank you."*

Anytime you catch yourself feeling powerless or victimized, then strengthen the belief that you are the creator of your reality. No matter what is happening, how you are being treated, or how powerless you feel to change certain aspects in your life, you do have the authority. You have a choice and this is what you are choosing. Even though you cannot imagine how you would be choosing what you are experiencing. Telling yourself this will help you take responsibility in understanding that you are the creator of your life. Take time to recognize the decisions you made that created the situation you are in. You do not need others to give you what you want. You and your higher self can create any life you dream of. The power of the mind can paint these wonders and bring it to fruition. Having one negative thought will negate and block it from happening. Quickly tell your Spirit team to cancel the negative thought you had and replace it with a positive affirmation. Keep your vibrational energy high!

Avoid getting caught up in depressing feelings surrounding where you're currently at. There are positives to every situation. If you're feeling dispirited, then look at the hidden blessings in your current reality. Okay, so you are not happy at your job and you want to leave or move into a position within the company that has more meaning to you. Change your thought vibrations to highlight something positive. For example, feel thankful that you have a job to begin with, and that your bills are paid. By shifting the vibration of your thoughts into something optimistic, you invite that energy in! It will not be long before you do get the job, career, relationship, or home you want. After shifting your thoughts into something positive, then take little action steps towards making your dream happen.

It is not enough to remain optimistic and positive. This is a vital aspect, yes, but you must also pay attention to your Spirit team's messages and guidance intended to lead you to your ultimate goal. You need to take the action steps they put in front of you in order to create a dent towards your dream. Investigate and research the areas of your interest, then dive on in. When you are healthy and clear minded, then you raise your vibration. Raising your vibration opens up the channels of communication to your Spirit team on the other side. They show you the next steps by handing you little opportunities that propel you one move closer to your dream. When you are dispirited, then you do not notice the messages of assistance. Be happy and optimistic in believing that you have everything you want now. This positive view opens your world right up. Many of the Archangels can assist you with this. Call upon Archangel Raphael to elevate your mood when it takes a dip into pessimism. Call on Archangel Michael when you're experiencing fear. Call on Archangel Raziel to assist you in manifesting your dreams.

# Chapter Six

## DISCONNECTING AND ELIMINATING

Are you putting more focus and attention into your professional life leaving your personal life neglected? If one area in your life gets more attention than the other, then you have created an imbalance. When this happens, you are more inclined to remain stressed out, tired, and irritable. My Spirit team emphasizes on keeping your life in balance. Do this by honing in on the two most popular areas of your life: Home and work. This is the personal and professional.

Disconnect from the world as often as possible to clear your mind. Running your body into overdrive causes an array of health issues that are not limited to daily burn out. Disconnecting from your computer and phone for a few hours at a time is a great way to start. An even better way if possible is doing this for an entire day at least once a week. Use that time to interact with yourself or a close one such as a friend, your family or relationship partner. Hanging out with someone who is negative, toxic or feeds an addiction is not using the disconnection wisely. If you are going to use the disconnection time to put in quality time with a loved one, ensure that it is someone who is optimistic, joyful and makes healthy life choices.

Avoid bringing your work home, or your personal life to work. You manage your soul and body. Only you know what area in your life is lopsided or receives little to no attention. Take charge and personally manage your day. If you are working too much, then take some vacation time off, even if it is a day or two a month. Focusing heavily on your interpersonal relationships and home life causes strain. Find a hobby or activity you enjoy doing that is productive. Make sure you keep your home and work life balanced otherwise you will experience symptoms of burn out.

## STAY AWAY FROM NOISE

I do not pay much attention to the news, media and gossip sites. It is typically days after a major story has hit the news when I hear about it through the grapevine. By this time, it has already been going on awhile. I discover that the world is in an uproar over something ridiculous or gossipy. I say ridiculous because all is always well. No one truly cares about the story since it's not long before they've shifted their focus onto the next attention grabbing headline. The uproars and the lynch mob mentality behavior are products of human ego. They serve no one and benefit nothing. All it does is add negativity and suppressed, blocked energy onto the planet. Human ego loves to create drama and issues out of a story. This goes for those that soak themselves into a story reacting to it negatively in some manner. Other responsible parties are those who work in the media feeding it to the masses like poison. The stories have a design intended to get a rise out of you and work you up into a panicked or angry frenzy. When in the end, everything works itself out the way it's intended. There will always be something new in the media that pops up to suddenly divert everybody's focus onto the latest scandal, end of the world talk, or court trial. Yet they have ironically forgotten all about what they were upset about a week before that had meant so much to them at the time. How do so many live their lives donating so much of their energy into useless noise? There is no point to that existence. This exhausts your energy and keeps you from doing something that benefits you, the planet, and its people in a positive way. Stay away from all of it and focus on what makes your heart sing and brings you or others joy.

If you notice that you are feeling agitated, then the best thing to do is to make immediate soul enhancement steps. Think of what relaxes you or brings you joy. Head immediately to your nearest nature locale where there is little to no people. Breathe in all of that beautiful nature, the trees, grass, flowers, and ask God to surround you with angels creating a healing love cushion. Ask that they extract any negative ions that have latched onto your loving spirit.

If your days have been particularly intense, you may say something like this: *"Dear God. Please surround me with a hundred angels today creating a cushion of love. Thank you."*

When I have said those words on a particularly severe day in the past, I would find that my day would alter from intense to breezing effortlessly through it afterwards.

Are you procrastinating? Are you feeling like you are running around in a circle heading nowhere? This is a clue that it is time to work on breaking away from the self-imposed prison you have constructed for yourself. Break away from running around in a circle and find another path to go down. Break away from anything that is holding you back from moving forward. You may need to go back and re-examine what it is you want and how it is you are going about in obtaining it. Look at what needs modifying in your life. Take that new enlightened information and run with it. Shine a light on specific areas in your life that you are not paying attention to that need some revisions. Those adjustments will lead you towards the Sun and the happiness you crave.

## FULL MOON RELEASING

Release that which has been delaying you and holding you back from positive progress. You likely already know what you need to let go of, but are procrastinating out of fear or indecision. It is anything or anyone that brings you down or prompts you to experience consistent inadequate feelings such as depression, anger or stress. This also includes foods and substances that are not good for you and cause your body to react negatively such as giving you low energy or irritability. This delays you from taking positive action and in moving forward. Release anything negative so that you can truly be free and soar upwards to where your higher self lives. When you release negative stuff, then you are on your way to obtaining your dreams. Your dreams come true as a result of this release, but you have to do the work. You have to release negative thoughts, patterns, lifestyle choices and people.

The Full Moon transit which happens once a month is a great time for releasing, re-aligning and then manifesting (positively - so watch your thoughts!) Many use the night of the Full Moon to release that which no longer serves them or their higher self. Release anything or anyone that you know is toxic and causes you to experience uncomfortable feelings. The energy of the Full Moon is potent, intense, and powerful. It brings up all sorts of feelings and thoughts. It has the power to magnify and direct your energy in large ways. This is why it is important to be crystal-clear with your thoughts in general, and especially on the night of the Full Moon.

Simply having intention can make this release happen efficiently. One way is by meditating or gazing upon the Full Moon for 5-15 minutes. Take a deep breath in, exhale, and repeat until you are fully relaxed. Breathe in and connect with the Moon so that you are one with it. You can do this longer than 15 minutes if you choose. Sitting underneath the Full Moon outside in order to make contact with you is even better. Sometimes this is not realistic if it is a cloudy or rainy night, but as long as the intention is there is all that matters. Mentally visualize what you would like to remove from your life. Follow that with what you would like to see come to fruition. This brings in your Spirit team by your side notating the work you are putting in to make healthy life changes. Archangel Haniel is the hierarchy angel who you can benefit from working with. Ask her to be with you through this Full Moon releasing process. She awakens your third eye chakra which opens up clairvoyance.

# Flowers

Flowers raise your vibration, so fill your surroundings with flowers. Purchase flowers or put up photographs of flowers. Having the real thing is the most beneficial. If the only option is a framed picture of a flower due to severe allergies or other circumstances, then that is better than no flowers. If you have allergies, call on Archangel Raphael and ask him to reduce or eliminate the severity of the allergies. Pay attention to the guidance he places in your path where other alternatives to having a flower can come into play.

Lean into the flower and breathe it in. If this is a photograph of a flower, then envision that it is real as you lean in to breathe it in. Notice how wide open the flower is with its arms outstretched. Take it all in allowing it to awaken and open up your mind and senses. Meditate on the flower or image and take a deep breath in. On the exhale release any negative thoughts or lower vibration words that you have been using. The flower's arms expand wide giving you a big hug.

The flowers, trees, grass and all of nature are gifts from God to help you relax and connect with your Spirit team. God created flowers for numerous purposes. One of them is to surround you with beauty. Beauty and flowers both raise your vibration. It's a double whammy! It is not okay to destroy nature and this world through greed and naivety. Flowers keep this planet alive and to keep you feeling alive. Flowers are little reminders of the beauty that exists in the Spirit world, which is abundantly ripe with flowers. Nature is a powerful sense awakener with immense healing properties. When you take in a huge inhale of a flower, you feel invigorated. Your mind opens up becoming clear, focused and stimulated. Absorbing nature regularly prompts you to experience the natural uplifting feelings of well-being.

Placing flowers around you can invite positive circumstances into your life. Each color tends to bring in specific energy into your vicinity. The darker the shade of that particular color, then the more intense it will be. The lighter the shade of that color, then the softer the energy will be. If it is a pink flower, it can bring in more love into your life. If that pink is a deeper rose color, then the love will be heavier, more intense. The lighter the pink is in that flower, then the softer the love is or subtle it is.

Here is an example cheat sheet of the healing properties that the color of a flower can give off. Place these flowers around your space if you would like to invite in a higher energy for a specific desire:

- ❖ *Red* – passion, romance, sexiness, deep relationships and commitments
- ❖ *Pink* – Love, beauty, attractiveness
- ❖ *Yellow* – Joy, optimism, success, ideas, thoughts, friendships
- ❖ *Green* – Healing, releasing, cleansing
- ❖ *Violet* – Spiritual awakenings, protection, third eye opening
- ❖ *White* – Harmony, Purity, vibration lifting, hope
- ❖ *Orange* – Growth, empowerment, expansiveness, career
- ❖ *Blue* – Strength, courage, calming, honor, creativity

There are books available on the market devoted to flowers that can offer more detail and insight into the healing properties that exist. Do an Internet search and type in something like: 'flower therapy'.

## Your Light Is Power

Show your best self by sharing your light with others on a daily basis. Let it out and let it shine bright. This inspires a mighty movement of peace. The hardness and toxicity that has plagued humankind for so long is outdated. The light exists inside of you. You must allow it to take back the control of your surroundings. Be a warrior of light. Do your best to stay in that space even when you stumble upon a roadblock or a difficult human soul. Demanding people are merely acting out from their ego, which has no power or validity with anything real or long lasting.

The ego lives in fear and acts out in fits of temper much like a child having an outburst when it doesn't get what it wants. You find peace, joy, strength and love when you remain centered in the light. When you lose your way, ask for heavenly assistance to get back on track. The more you ask for help and work with your Spirit team to reach this space of contentment, then the easier it gets. What can work for you might be lighting a candle and meditating on this light. Call in your Spirit team to begin the process of re-aligning your soul. Empty out your negative thoughts as you focus on this candlelight. Close your eyes and envision that the flame of the light is taking over any negative thoughts and blasting it away while lifting it off your body. Make room in your consciousness to receive the messages coming in from Spirit to help you be at peace and feel encompassed by love.

I have crossed paths with a wide variety of people who have different belief systems and values. I have witnessed those who might disagree with any of this or who find it to be ineffective. Yet, these are the same people that struggle in a constant uphill battle. Or they might be the ones who have been stagnant with no hope for escape. When in those states, your ego dominates your life big time ensuring that you never progress. Within you is the knowledge of all lifetimes. Within you is the knowledge of why you are here. Pay attention to your intuition as that is one of the many barometer gauges that exist within your soul that accurately receives heavenly messages. All human souls receive heavenly communication everyday without exception. It is irrelevant what the soul's personal values and beliefs are, and whether they're aware that it is indeed their Guides and Angels. Pay attention to the messages in order to help you navigate through life much easier than if you were not aware of them.

Keeping your vibration high takes daily work. It's a lifestyle and view change you're adopting. One day you are riding on cloud nine with joy, which raises your vibration. Your vibration remains high until a negative thought enters your mind thus causing it to take a tip again. The next day you go on a drinking binge. This drinking binge prompts your vibration to drop astronomically. It can be a struggle to raise it than it is to drop it. Raising it back up can feel like pushing a huge boulder up a steep hill. Those privy to this knowledge can raise their vibration much easier than someone unaware of what to do in order to get it there. Having an interfering culprit like the ego is what gets its kicks out of double-crossing you and ensuring your vibration stays low. It makes sure that you do not succeed. When you make a commitment to incorporating higher vibration methods into your life every day, then you will notice the changes in your life shifting in a more positive direction.

# Chapter Seven

## THE POWER OF LOVE AND RELATIONSHIPS

The only thing that matters in the end is love. It is the #1 reason you are here. All souls have this love gene within them. Everyone has the gift and ability to love and express love, yet so many stop living in this space full time. They give or expect love with peculiar conditions behind it. If you do not feel love or do not have any love to give, then take steps to elevating your consciousness. Do not allow the wrath of your ego to dominate your behavior. The ego has no love. Any love that it does show has an ulterior motive behind it. This motive aligns with qualities such as greed or betrayal. It will crush your spirit and turn you into something cold - which is also a front. I have witnessed this happen in others where past circumstances have caused them to shut down from giving and receiving love. They are unable to be intimate in their relationships or in friendships. This is unfathomable to me. Love and joy are the highest vibrations that exist. Love is the nourishment that keeps your soul riding on cloud nine. It keeps you healthy and lucky in attracting in positive circumstances to you. Make a pact to live in the space of love full time.

A potential love partner comes to you when you least expect it. All of the serious relationships I have had in my past happened when I was not looking for it. Each one of them came about in the same manner. It did not happen when I was purging, in the middle of a change, or other major internal transformation. These soul mates showed up after I had gone through a mini-shift, which allowed me to experience peace. I was in a place of total contentment when every one of my romantic soul mates entered my life. As a love addict, I've always been consumed with an overflowing feeling of love. Growing up, I would use my pillow as if it were the one I was with. I would daydream of falling asleep with someone and having a profound connection with them in a loving, committed relationship. By the time I was sixteen, I was ready to unite with a soul mate in a marriage for life. I am a love bug and place the bar high when it comes to all things love.

Before the days of technology, relationships lasted throughout the duration of the couples Earthly lives. People stayed together and worked at it. There was less materialistic ego getting in the way that has a habit of crumbling the connections today. There is no perfect partner and yet through my research and interviews with single people, I've discovered that many of them are seeking perfection. This is a time in the world that is dangerously fixated on the media, fads and sexually charged images. Newer generations learn about this instant gratification desire. Fed to them since birth, they absorb this illusion and ultimately meet disappointment head on. There is perfection created in the media and in these images. They display false interpretations of reality. This is with the use of great lighting, camera angles, make-up and hair people toying with the one in front of the camera to make them look out of this world. Having worked in the entertainment industry for a good chunk of my life, and raised in the business, I have seen how they orchestrate everything to create the perfect shot. Most people have admitted to touching up their own "selfies" before posting those photos on social media. This is connected to self esteem issues that have risen in astronomical numbers in others due to the internet's perception that everyone must be picture perfect. What happens when you meet these picture perfect photo people in person for the first time? Both of you are not exactly what you expected each other to look like and therefore you've wasted one another's time. The sole reason you met them to begin with was you expected a flawless appearing human being who looks as if they jumped right out of a fashion magazine.

All souls are shifting in and out of each other's lives for numerous purposes. Soul connections made have no set period in how long they last. They might last a week, months, years or even a lifetime and beyond. Some come into your life so that you can learn important life lessons that prompt you to change and grow. This is where the connection might be a challenging one, but in the end it enhances your soul pending you learn valuable lessons from the connection. It must happen or you would not be ready for the next big step. You connect with that person in order to join forces with them on a particular quest or to gain specific knowledge. They may be your soul brother or sister. You connect through several lifetimes sometimes just to say hello.

## MESSAGES ON LOVE

Sometimes you overlook the potential suitors sent your way. They may not be the kind of person you were expecting so you do not bother with getting to know them. You do not feel like you have a shot. When you run into this person, you instead avoid them. Your own Spirit team sets up these chance encounters. They work together with the other person's guardian angel and spirit guide in order to orchestrate a meeting or a place where you will both cross paths. They will not bring a romantic soul mate into your life to replace your current one. If you meet someone while with your current mate, this does not necessarily mean your Spirit team sent this person. Heaven is about working it out with your current mate before considering bringing another into your life. Your current relationship would have to end. Time would need to be spent working on yourself afterwards before a new soul mate is delivered to you.

There is one exception. For some, they have a lifelong soul mate or twin flame relationship that will come to them regardless if they are already in a relationship. This is because you and this other soul chose to meet at such and such time no matter what. It was set up and designed long before you were born into an Earthly life. You will know this is the soul mate if you end up with this person for the duration of both of your Earthly lives.

It can be challenging, because many people do not follow the guidance of their Guides and Angels and may be more prone to act on free will. There will be times where you or this other potential does not happen, because one or the both of your egos refuse it. Your Spirit team will continue with the search of putting other potential possibilities in your path hoping you both notice each other and strike up a conversation. They will at times continue to put the same person in your path for months and maybe even years trying to get you two to notice one another if it is indeed meant to happen this lifetime. This is why some couples have later recounted that after they became acquainted with one another they indeed had some near misses. They discover they had many missed encounters where they would have been together much sooner if it were not for their ego denying it or the fault of poor timing. Perhaps they were at the same store location, but missed each other by a couple of minutes. They can be the two people who work in the same building together, but continue to miss one another in the lobby and elevator by mere minutes. These unforeseen circumstances cause long delays between soul mates meeting and uniting. You and your potential soul mates Guides and Angels can only maneuver and control so much in order to get you two to connect. It's challenging for them to work on delaying or speeding up morning traffic in such a way that you both manage to arrive at the work building at the same time. They do indeed perform these brilliant miracles, but this is to illustrate the amount of challenging circumstances they have to move around to get you both in the same elevator together.

I receive questions from others regarding personal psychic or angel reading sessions they had with a reader. Sometimes the question might be regarding messages they received from their own Guides and Angels. One of the questions is they are told that they are meant for a specific person in a relationship, but that the person in question is already involved with someone else. The answer is an easy one. He/she may not last with this other person. When it is complete, then you will both cross paths and merge, pending that no other circumstances have taken place with either party. Two human souls who are meant to have a soul mate connection with each other will cross paths with one another repeatedly over a lengthy period of time until they finally notice one another and take action. If they do not take action, there are several reasons for this below.

There are people who are supposed to meet each other and yet they never manage to connect in this lifetime. This is mostly due to free will. Most human souls have saturated themselves into the material world. The media, their peers, and society heavily influence their nature. This blocks the important messages and guidance coming in from the spirit world. This makes that person more susceptible to ruling from their ego. For that matter, they tend to act upon free will. When you act upon free will, then you miss the gifts and wonders that God is placing in your higher path including a beautiful all encompassing love relationship.

When it comes to two people connecting in a soul mate relationship, one or the both of you acts on free will and denies that the person they have crossed paths with is the one. Their ego convinces them that the soul mate potential is not what they are attracted to. They write off behavior patterns or habits this person does without giving them a fair chance. There are habits in others that are an understandable definite no such as they drink heavily, do drugs, stray, sleep around and hang out in bars regularly as a fixture. The habits I am talking about are much smaller and forgivable such as they did not return your text immediately that day. Or they are not tall, blonde and built to the nines. Your ego quickly writes them off, not realizing that this person is the one you are to connect with in this lifetime.

Before the media took over and dominated its influence on humanity, there was a courting process between two people. The couple in question was much more accepting of the other's idiosyncrasies and foibles. They also took their time getting to know one another before anything physical happened. This not only made the physical emerging sexier and hotter, but it also contributed to the longevity of their connection. The connections today are immediate and fleeting. This prompts many couples to split long before they truly know each other.

You cannot call one a couple or say that they are in a long-term relationship until they have been together for at least a year. Half of the couples that connect today do not make it that long. This creates a combination of loneliness and aloofness among souls whose basic nature is supposed to be love. This makes you grow cold and detached while continuing with your search for something instant to give you immediate pleasure and satisfaction. All the while wondering what it would be like to be with someone in a long-term marriage like relationship. Years pass and this pattern in your life increases to an astronomical and unmanageable degree. The image of this soul mate connection starts to take on a picture perfect vision that makes it even harder to believe it will come true. The person you seek and which you have conjured up in your mind has perfect qualities that no one in the world could fulfill. This perpetuates and delays any connection to any potential soul mate partner.

When you are in a relationship, be unlimited in love. I used to say that I was difficult in love. Due to my past relationship experiences, I assumed the love I demanded was over the top or outlandish to a degree because I discovered no one knew how to do it. The intensity is beyond what an ordinary human being can give, but those who are no ordinary human souls understand this. Sent here with our individual purposes that have the capacity to be far reaching, one can find disappointment in ordinary human soul love. Our hearts are just too big for our body to contain. The truth is the right one has the same equal belief systems, values and desires as you do. It is the same give and take. You cannot allow the quality and size of your Spirit to squeeze itself into a limited system of values. You are whole, perfect and full of immense love. Allow this to shine so bright that it attracts in the right mate for you. Be completely together much more than you realize! Get out there and continue to live life. Go to the places you want to go and do not allow anyone to stop you from living and loving. Let go of the need to control the need to know when the soul mate connection will happen. Trust it is evolving on divine timing.

Know that some soul mates are an awakener for you. This is by allowing you to experience the emotions and thoughts that you had unknowingly closed off. The soul mates purpose is to bring your true soul out of the human body to get some air!

## CHEMISTRY

Having chemistry with another human soul is only the beginning of where it could potentially lead if anywhere. This is a comfortably, strong and deep attraction that is experienced by both people when they are together. Chemistry is a positive mutual, reciprocated feeling with another person. You cannot act on chemistry alone though.

Having chemistry on a first meeting with someone is natural for any human soul who is connecting to the newness of someone you have crossed paths with. This does not mean it is meant to move forward beyond that. Chemistry can be a dangerous thing depending on the scenario. Human souls are always experiencing chemistry with other souls, but that does not mean it is a love relationship waiting to happen. You can have chemistry with your closest friends and that is all it is, a friendship.

There are many different levels of chemistry. There is the, "I just want to have sex with this person", chemistry. There is the, "This person really gets me on a friend level", kind of chemistry. A successful relationship experiences chemistry on many levels. You are physically attracted to each other. This person is also your friend. Drawn to one another you find yourself heading back to that person and they are drawn to you.

Being with someone who is exactly like you in every way can lead the relationship to grow stale. This works for friendships that you communicate with on a regular basis, but not so much love relationships, which require some shades that are slightly different from your partner. The hues are not vastly different where it causes constant friction of course, but different enough that it continues to attract you to this other person. They are not quite like you, but there are elements about them that pull you in. Although it is important to have similar interests and values to an extent, it is even more so important that both parties involved in the relationship have some differences. This is somewhat close to the saying that claims opposites attract. The fine print version of the opposites attract syndrome is that they should not be too much of an opposite because then you will not connect completely. An extrovert can indeed be in a healthy long-term relationship with someone who is an introvert as long as they are facing the same direction. This is a case of opposites attract working.

One of the many reasons love relationships happen is for

the sake of your soul's growth. For this reason, being involved in a healthy long-term relationship is beneficial when you are with someone who has some elemental differences than you. You will gain knowledge and lessons from this soul. It will also teach you to love someone who is not exactly like you. The relationship in general will teach you to work with others through compromise and communication. These are life lessons that build character and thus enhance your soul's growth.

There does come a point where the differences might be too vast for a relationship to thrive. These are what might seem obvious in the realms of common sense. If someone is incredibly different from you on every level, then coming together might be impossible. This is not the case if it is a sexual connection. Human souls do experience the kind of chemistry that takes place with someone you are simply lusting after in a sexual way. Anyone that has partaken in such chemistry knows that it is short-lived and not long lasting. This is not to say you should stay away from that kind of connection. If you are one hundred percent single and alone, then there is nothing wrong with connecting in a physical way with someone you are having strong, intense feelings for sexually. Ensure you are being responsible and using safety precautions, but know that it will not assist you in finding the love you crave.

When strong feelings are involved, your dopamine levels rise. Dopamine is the naturally producing chemical in the brain that prompts you to display loving feelings. Being a Don Juan Casanova type myself, I have met no other who knows about breathing in this dangerous chemical full time. What is hazardous about it is if you target this love towards someone who is wrong for you. Having this feeling for someone you meet while currently with someone in a relationship is not for the right reasons. The Romance Angels say that taking off in search of greener pastures is like chasing rainbows that eventually fade. The love chemical in your brain can cause you to see things with rose-colored glasses. It is unsafe to your heart when you direct this towards someone who does not share this same love with you. While there is nothing wrong with loving love, keep some measure of a reality in check so that you do not get hurt.

When you have chemistry with someone at the beginning of getting to know them, you likely do not pay much attention to the red flags. Later when your union hits a wall of unhealthy issues, you look back in hindsight remembering how you did see the red flags. You failed to think much of it until you dove too deep into the connection. You might use the excuse of, "Well had I known this I never would've moved forward with the relationship. By the time I discovered all this, I was too emotionally attached." In truth, if you take a step back you might be able to hone in on where the red flags were apparent. It might've felt so subtle at the time that you failed to think much of it. Most human souls tend to have the rose colored glasses on when they experience immediate soul attraction to someone who is feeling the same thing. Rose colored glasses give you the great love high, but the mirrors of the glasses are fogged up to the point where the real reality is distorted.

If you are in a loving, committed relationship and a red flag pops up, that does not necessarily mean to leave the relationship. At that point, it is more about addressing an issue that is extreme enough to rock the foundation of your connection. Your partner is in the relationship with you at that point and should be open to working out whatever the issue is. If you notice they're flirtatious with others when you're out together, the chances are they were always flirtatious by nature. They don't suddenly become flirtatious way into your relationship.

Sometimes long-term relationships lose their chemistry, but if the couple was able to come together repeatedly over the course of time, then the chances are they can restore the chemistry and balance in the relationship. A long lasting relationship goes through highs and lows while they are together. They are fully aware they fall in and out of love with each other over the course of their life. Falling out of love does not mean hatred or leaving the relationship. It is having an understanding of the basic nature of the human ego, because your higher soul is all love and never falls out of love with anything or anyone. There will be periods of detachment between one another while in a committed relationship. Allow your partner the space they need and be willing to communicate about anything important. Knowing when the other person needs space is vital. The partner having a temporary moment of detachment could be going through a personal transition or transformation. The other partner senses this and grants them the required space, while remaining nearby should their mate need them. Any couple that takes their partnership seriously realizes that they may hit a wall where it feels as if the chemistry has evaporated. The partnership is strong and rock solid enough that one or both of them soon rise to the task to rekindle the fire that never truly extinguishes for good.

## INVITE LOVE INTO YOUR LIFE

Over the course of entertainment history, there have been love songs recorded, romantic movies filmed, and books written about having a secure, loving and passionate relationship. Someone felt those things, craved it, experienced it firsthand or witnessed it in others. Love is a universal need. It is your soul's innate nature even if you lost the ability to operate from that space. You can find that space again because the love you were born with never leaves. You just bury it beneath layers of cement.

Many singles feel discouraged about love. They crave and desire it, but when pining for a wonderful soul mate has turned to years of rejection or no success, then it can cause one to become everlastingly disappointed. The Romance

Angels say that remaining optimistic about love is what is going to bring you this love. I can attest personally that I understand how difficult that can be, but through work you can get there. Doing the work means catching yourself when you find that you are negative whenever it comes to the word love. Be aware when this happens and then shift your state of mind into something positive.

Think something like, "I am blessed with a loving, soul mate relationship." Say it as if it is already here. It's about believing that it is happening now, rather than it's going to happen. Nothing is going to stop you from obtaining it. Get into the joy of your life. Feel the feelings of optimism when it comes to all aspects of your life. This opens up your heart chakra to receive love. When you are playful, lighthearted, joyful, and allow your inner child to shine, then you will attract in wonderful soul mates to you.

One way to focus on love is when you head to sleep at night. You are lying down in bed as your thoughts drift. Allow your thoughts to move into a visualization of you in a relationship with the kind of person you envision yourself to be happy with. Picture yourself in the house together with the picket fence and the animals. Go all out and do not withhold for fear of it not happening, or that you are being what someone's ego might call cliché. This is about you. What do you desire? Allow your mind to play you this mini-movie of this relationship you seek. It may come to you quickly or it may take some time, but never give up on love. Love yourself and those around you more. Become more appreciative of having these loving thoughts.

You can purchase some Rose Quartz crystals and leave it next to your bed. You can also put it under your pillow when you sleep. Carry it in your pocket, car, or purse. Lie down on your back somewhere comfortable in meditation and place this crystal on your heart. Take a deep breath in and exhale, then repeat this step as you relax. Visualize the crystal opening up your heart and allowing love to pour into your heart. Envision this love pouring back out of your heart and into your love's soul light across from you. Allow the light to envelope the both of you. It is not necessary to have a specific vision of what this person looks like and in fact it will be equally powerful allowing them to be faceless. This means you're leaving the door open for the angels to bring you a soul mate who might be more amazing than you initially imagined.

Purchase some *rose essential oil* and dab it on your heart. This is beneficial when you have been feeling closed off from others. Breathe in deeply and see a magical pink light shooting into your heart from Heaven. Send this light out tenfold back upwards and out of your body like a geyser. It is not necessary to go all out and purchase Rose Quartz crystals or rose essential oil, but it most certainly will not hurt it. You can manifest what you want with the power of your own mind. Love will come. Love is here. Love is within you and always will be.

Love yourself more in order to open up the feelings of love within and around you. This can be in the form of self-love, which is admiring all that you are. Love how you physically appear. Strip down and look at yourself in the mirror and say, "I love my body." Buy yourself a gift as if you are buying it for someone you love. Watch a romantic movie, have a massage, some pampering at a spa, or take a mini-vacation somewhere. Dive into your hobbies that bring you joy. All of this is self-care, which not only opens up your heart chakra, but also assists you in bringing those love feelings to the surface. You glow in this state and other potential suitors or people on the street notice this. You are a magnet that attracts in love. If you are currently in a relationship, then this will add some extra love into your connection. Even more powerful is if your partner participates in this with you.

Keep in mind that sometimes the soul mate you envision or crave may appear in a different way. They might be right in front of you and yet you are not immediately noticing. This is because you have a specific vision of who you think they will be that you do not realize that this soul mate is already in your vicinity. They may not be what you were expecting and you might not even be completely attracted to them right away. There will be some measure of attraction, but it is so slight you write it off because you are not feeling all of the feelings you expect to happen with a potential soul mate. Those feelings grow even more as you get to know this soul mate. Keep an open heart and an open mind while on your search for a love companion. Release the need to know when or how this person will come to you. Find activities that make you smile and enjoy. This keeps your heart wide open. You will be so busy enjoying yourself only to discover your soul mate has arrived and you are having a conversation. Worrying about when or how it will happen darkens your aura, causes you grief, and prompts you to feel depressing thoughts. This does not make your light attractive to others and you certainly do not want to repel your soul mate from entering your vicinity.

If you have had a history of bad past relationships, use the time that you are single to make crystal clear intentions about what you will or will not accept in a loving, relationship. You will want to keep these needs somewhat flexible. If you are too rigid in your list, then you will repel the right soul mate for you. The kinds of things that are understandable of what you will not accept are things like, cheating, abuse in any form, alcohol or drug addictions, etc. The list would not include things such as where you insist that your soul mate calls you back immediately whenever you send a text. Controlling demands do not invite a loving, compassionate and loyal partner to you. It instead brings in a partner who exudes the negative traits you were hoping they would not have in them to begin with.

In this same respect, controlling your current relationship if you are in one creates a difficult situation. No one likes to be controlled or have harsh demands placed on their backs. If your current partner is behaving in ways that you disagree with or that do not jive with your values, then discussing it peacefully with them is the next step. If that does not work, then consider working with a couple's counselor. It also boils down to what you can live with. If your current partner is not abusive, or addicted to alcohol or drugs, and does not cheat, then put in some extra effort to work on the partnership before considering leaving. If you leave, you will find that you will be stuck with someone far worse than your current mate is.

When making a commitment to someone else, you are first making a commitment to you. This practice of commitment with your own self is what you will carry over into your loving companionship with your partner. If you are irresponsible in your own life, with your actions and decisions, then you are not quite ready to commit to another human soul. This shows if you have a tendency towards short-lived connections that have no staying power. Work on taking responsibility for your life, yourself, your soul and all of your surroundings. Making a shift in that direction where it becomes second nature to you is what will make it that much more effortless when joining with another committed, loving soul.

While in a relationship, avoid divulging every little tidbit that goes wrong with those close to you such as your friends. They may persuade you to leave a divinely orchestrated relationship. The natural reaction from those close to you is that they will side with you and not your partner. This is unfair to the person you are with. It will cause you more confusion when you are influenced by the words of those close to you. You have no idea what action to take if any. If it has come to that, it is best to take a time out for yourself and disconnect temporarily from your circle until you have individual perspective.

Loving relationships that run into roadblocks or a stalemate can deepen their connection by spending time alone together. This means getting away for a weekend trip or hiding out in your house and creating a romantic environment for just the two of you. When you spend time alone with your partner, then your feelings grow. This is extra beneficial for a relationship that has reached a point where one or the both of you feel stuck. This is what it means when others say relationships take work. You have to put in the work. You have to care about it. When you care about your relationships, then you care about you.

I am a firm believer of date night at least once a week while in a relationship. Inject laughter and fun on your date nights. It should be a relaxed and playful time for the both of you to forget any cares, stresses or worries around you. Love relationships have this benefit in that the right partnership is an escape from all negativity in the world. When you are with them, you remember what is truly important in this life. Love is all that matters. Loving relationships help you remember your divine heritage.

## Chapter Eight

## THE SECRETS TO SUCCESSFUL RELATIONSHIPS

Most human souls desire companionship on some level. You crave someone to be by your side that understands and supports you. Someone you champion and who appreciates you in return. For some, it might be a platonic friendship, for others it might be a sexual relationship with the same person throughout this lifetime. Your soul split into two souls at its original conception. This other half of you is your twin flame who many long for. They are a part of you, although not everyone connects with their twin flame in this lifetime. You move through this life feeling like there is something missing. In essence, you are searching for your twin flame. For most human souls, their twin flame is usually on the other side guiding you to healthy soul mate relationships for you on your Earthly journey.

Jaded singles have protested a myth that they believe those who are in relationships are unhappy. This could not be further from the truth. Those in unhappy or volatile relationships usually contain one or both partners who are not ready for a real relationship. They have not done the inner work yet. They bring their worst selves, their ego, and negative habits into the relationship, and then place that burden onto their partner. The connection is full of toxic energy that never lets up. The couple might be the type that argues more than they express love. It is normal to have a disagreement with your partner, but it is harmful if you are butting heads on a regular basis. Those who are in successful committed relationships are happier, healthier and more productive in their lives than those who are not in peaceful connections. The ingredients for a successful long-term relationship are vast.

One of the secrets to happy relationships is that both partners are open and communicative with one another. If you do not communicate openly, then how do you expect your partner to know what your needs are? How are you to work at it if your partner has no idea how you are feeling? Meanwhile, you are making plans that will affect your mate and they have no idea. It is not fair to leave the one you are involved with in the dark.

When you head to work or your job, you have to do more than show up. You actually have to do the work. Granted you are receiving money to do that work. Whereas in a relationship the payment you receive is the experience and lessons you gain with your partner that benefit your soul's growth. This is worth far more than any money earned. Money is temporary, while your soul lasts forever.

Another problem that can arise is that you or your partner feels uncomfortable or afraid to bring something serious up with the other one. This is not being assertive, but living in fear. You might fear that your partner will take it the wrong way or that they might attack you if you bring a concern up. If your partner always attacks you for opening up, then this is a red flag that you are with the wrong person. No one should have to endure any measure of abuse from anyone ever. If there is an issue at your job, most people have to bring it up unless they want it to blow up in their face down the line. If they do not bring it up, then disaster will hit. Someone will say, "This could have been prevented." Alternatively, they might say, "Why wasn't I notified?" In relationships, some couples are afraid to bring serious needs and issues up because they do not want to rock the boat. If you do not bring your concerns up or any potential issues, it is not going to go away. In fact, it will grow into a bigger problem resulting in more damage.

Your relationships are to be safe haven. You need to feel most at home when you are with your mate. You should be feeling safe enough to communicate openly and work through issues together by talking it out and taking action steps to mend what needs to be. Not being able to talk to your partner about anything is like walking on broken glass. This is no way to live a healthy and happy life.

You have been feeling suspicious that your partner is not being faithful. You do not want to mention this insecurity because you fear that you will be wrong. You worry that your partner will judge you, criticize you, get defensive or attack you for the accusation. This is not a loving partner. A loving partner is understanding and compassionate. They reassure you that there is nothing going on with anyone else and that you have nothing to fear. If your partner does become angry and defensive, then this can potentially be an admission of guilt. They are uncomfortable with emotional vulnerability and therefore not completely equipped to being in a loving, healthy relationship. On the other side of that equation, there is a difference between making a cruel accusation in anger and peacefully discussing insecure feelings. When you attack your partner, they will naturally become defensive and retaliate. All of this hostile energy flying back and forth, but no honest discussion with answers ever enters the equation. The ego of both partner's end up controlling the conversation leading you both nowhere, except more defeated and drained.

Those in successful relationships feel openly comfortable to discuss the touchy subjects such as vulnerabilities or insecurities in the relationship. They nip it in the bud immediately so that it does not grow like a dangerous, toxic weed in their beautiful garden.

Successful couples have similar values and interests to a degree. For example, both partners have a desire to live in the same part of town. You will run into problems if one of you wants to live in the big city around people, while the other prefers a quiet nature setting somewhere in a rural area or countryside.

If one partner feels like they cannot keep their feet planted in one spot and the other is perfectly at home doing that, then you will run into problems. There is a limit to how far compromise can go on some of these bigger issues. This is where communication is key once again.

Relationships are work and it is like a job in the sense that you both have to show up for the task. There are many couples where one is always on the go for weeks on end, while the other is at the home base. Is the one at the home base okay with this scenario? What if the partner on the go decides to take off and never come back? Is this who you want to commit to? There are billions of people in the world and it is impossible not to connect with someone who shares your ideals to an extent. You will find another soul mate potential with similar values as you have. This would include offering you more stability or reassurance that they are in this with you.

A successful relationship is facing in the same direction. It is joining to fight for everything around you together whether that is a parking ticket or having your partner's back in support.

Having or adopting children is another area where compromise does not always work. One of you wants or has plans to have children one day, while the other partner vocally does not or is flip floppy about it. This is where they protest that they want children, but then on another occasion they reveal they never had any interest in wanting kids. You are stunned to discover this truth. You could have sworn they were interested in having kids one day, while your partner is wondering how you ever got that idea in your mind. This type of person is flip floppy around many issues surrounding ones values. Flip-floppiness is someone who is not fully committed. They do not know what they want. Unfortunately, they are more or less stringing you along. You stay with them thinking they will change or that they need more time. Years in you come to the realization that they are never going to change or settle down. They have fears that govern their relationship lives and connecting with other people. This prevents them from being a grown up and mature soul. Fear is a relationship killer.

Human souls grow and evolve, but not always. Many stay relatively the same. When you were sixteen dreaming of a long-term committed relationship, this will not change when you are thirty-five. You more or less will still want that if it hasn't arrived or if you are newly single again. The only change would be that you grow more realistic as you age.

Trust is another important factor in a successful relationship, but more importantly is communication. Successful relationships endure because both partners communicate with one another and think of each other as the other's soul mate. Their love and understanding grows over time instead of fizzling out the way a fickle connection might. They are supportive of one another. They accept each other for who they are - imperfections and all. They work together in assisting in one another's growth. They shower one another with love and compassion. They are a beautiful and magnificent team.

Heaven and the angels love seeing two human souls in loving, committed relationships regardless of the genders involved. They know that once you are in a relationship that the real work enters the picture. They are by the sides of couples that request their assistance in empowering and improving the relationship. When there is friction going on or a disagreement between the both of you, then call on your Spirit team to intervene and mend the relationship. You can pray to God to send an angel to help your relationship. Assigned to your case will be the right angel or spirit guide. You may also call on Archangel Raguel who restores balance in relationships that are suddenly off kilter. He can mend any arguments or rifts that have risen. He will bring peace to all parties involved. Archangel Raguel is happy to do this for any type of connection, whether it is a love mate, friendship or colleague.

# Chapter Nine

## STAGES OF COUPLEDOM

Have you been in a situation where you are dating someone new and yet you have no idea what you are? By what you are, I mean are you dating, are you friends or are you in a relationship? What is the scenario? Many have professed uncertainty surrounding the appropriate title. They feel as if they are sitting in the dark not knowing what they are to the person whose company they enjoy. They might see the person they are dating as a good friendship, yet the connection feels like it is slightly more than a friendship. This will cause confusion and future pain if you are not talking about it.

You should never assume that you are together, but at the same time, your connection does need to be established. What if you are seeing someone who sees that you are both simply friends? You have wasted valuable time putting energy into a connection with someone who has no interest in a relationship. Another scenario would be that the other person feels you are in a relationship, and yet you do not. Therefore, you have been dating other people here and there while making a beeline to this other person who believes they are involved with you. This will also cause pain, heartache and damage to your connection. This kind of harm exists if one of you has more of an interest in your partnership and yet you carry on with it knowing this information. Edward was seeing Lisa regularly only to discover that there was never any clarity if they were together or not. They had been dating regularly for nearly a year at that point and had been intimate on top of that. Naturally, he assumed for that reason, that they were indeed an item. It turns out Lisa looked at the connection as if it were a friends with benefits union. She had been flirting with other people inappropriately outside of being with Edward.

The modern day world has come up with so many labels and tags to identify what people are that it feels like a buffet of noise. Labels are not important because two souls who operate on the same frequency know exactly what they are to one another. However, human souls feel more comfortable when they are able to identify what they are with this other person.

## DATING

Dating is a word that has lost its meaning. The latest fad that seems to have taken a rise within the newer generations specifically is that they feel uncomfortable using the word, *'dating'*. Dating might mean that this is serious and I might have to commit. There is a ton of fear about merging with another soul. Merging with other souls is one of the main reasons you are here. It is an instinctive need to connect with someone else. Instead of using the word dating, there are great amounts of people who use the phrase, *'hanging out.'* Using the phrase, *'hanging out'*, can and will cause confusion in a partnership that has not established what they are to begin with.

Dating is the process of getting to know someone

gradually to see if you are a relationship match. You are not getting married or entering a serious relationship with them. However, dating is what leads to the more serious titles. Some couples may date for a month and part their separate ways, while others may date for years. If you are 'hanging out' with this person, going to restaurants, doing things together and kissing and being intimate on any level, then you are dating. There is no way to run from that title. This is the definition of what dating is.

Those who use the phrase, 'hanging out', tend to bypass the essential dating stages. Instead, they rush into a relationship with someone else within a month of knowing them. This is not a relationship just because you change your social networking status to 'in a relationship'. You cannot define a real relationship as such in less than three months. Those that do so will find that the dating connection has ended sooner than when you began it. You should be dating for several months getting to know that person over time. This is where you discover their interests and what they are like. You are looking to see if this is someone that you could see yourself going the distance with in a real relationship for decades to come. Take it seriously and treat it with the utmost care. Having a blasé attitude about dating means you are not ready to merge into a serious connection with anyone. It is also giving you a clue that the outcome will be failure.

How far into your hanging out before you bring up the inevitable question about what you both are? What if you bring it up too soon and scare the other person away? One would hope that common sense would be evident that you are dating regardless. The rules that modern day society has made in terms of what you are, has left most people living in a fog.

If you are hanging out with another human soul regularly, being intimate, or the attraction is there on both ends, then you should refrain from hanging out with other people beyond a friendship. Unfortunately, not everyone observes that rule. The media, peers and society have decided to make up their own rules. This has contributed to chaotic confusion with love and relationships. Human souls have free will choice to do as they please. As creative as the numerous rules may be, unfortunately they do not ensure longevity for a long-term relationship. Nor do they teach a soul about unconditional love or working with another soul. Someone will feel left out or unsure. One or both parties will sabotage the connection at some point. Poor choices lead to a buildup of Karma on your life path. You need to have the talk and do it soon before it gets out of hand.

It was not this complicated before the 1970's and 1980's. This was before free love and the sexual revolution, which brought in its plusses and negatives in the process. Everyone grew to be free in a way that the courting process became too complex, dynamic and therefore much more chaotic. It was the end of long-term committed relationships as ego modernized souls would come to know it. Before that time, two souls would endure a lengthy courting process, which involved a form of hanging out. They felt and observed the sexual tension even if they had not kissed yet. You did not go out searching, chatting and hanging out with other potentials while courting someone. Doing so is bad form and having no integrity. This is what shows you someone's character. The Internet and phone apps that exist today connect everyone together, but they have also caused the relationship downfall. Technology did not shatter how relationships develop. It is the human ego, which has destroyed it. You give a child a new toy they are not ready to play with and you will have a problem. There are many who do not know how to properly court and date. Raised in a generation of texting, social networking, emailing, and phone apps have not helped with this. The ego wants more! It wants more friends, more people, more newness, more possibilities, more stimulation, more everything! The incessant search for immediate, self-gratifying, self-sabotaging sensations is a sign of detachment from your higher self, soul and God.

## Casually Dating Vs. Exclusively Dating

Define what you are together and agree on it. If you do not agree on it and neither of you is compromising, then you will run into issues.

Are you both going to agree that you are *Casually Dating* or are you *Exclusively Dating*?

**Casually Dating** means that you enjoy each other, but you are not serious or looking for anything serious. This is more or less someone you enjoy hanging out with. If either of you decided to stop it tomorrow, neither of you would care all that much. You may also be dating each other while dating other people casually as well. Of course, it is important that you are both on the same page that this is the set up you agreed on. Casually dating someone can be similar to a serial dater. This is someone who is always dating someone for a brief stint and then abruptly moves onto the next new person that enters their life. They are in love with the newness of someone. There are no hassles, no commitments and no responsibility needed. They are also chasing their tails. They may be dating several people at the same time or their dating scenarios with one person at a time are typically short-lived. They may also be the same people who add *'in a relationship'* to their social networking page status, even though they have just started dating that person. Within one to three months max they end up changing their social networking status back to *'single'*! They were never truly in a relationship to begin with. What they were doing was dating. They were never quite able to bring their dating situation to a REAL relationship efficiently. This is typically common with people younger than twenty-five who are inexperienced and tend to jump in immediately eliminating any essential courting process. It is not limited to someone under twenty-five as there are cases where people who are older do it as well. It is lacking in experience or having a deepened maturity level. This is a red flag, unless it is a scenario mutually agreed upon.

*Exclusively Dating* is where you are both loyal to one another through the dating process. You are incredibly interested in one another and you both want to see where it goes. You both imagined that you could be with this other person for life in a relationship. You are not dating around, seeing other people, or even chatting inappropriately with other people. You are investing time, energy and love into this person.

Dating can be tricky, because you do not immediately slap on the exclusively dating label, but it does happen fairly soon after a couple of months. You always start out with them as casually dating, but then as it continues to grow you are exclusively dating. You need to make sure that the other person is on the same page as you. This is the stage where you both may telepathically know you are an item, but you still have to clarify it. This should be easy for both as you are likely sharing much with one another to begin with. Exclusively dating one person is often termed also when the couple is not quite thinking of a serious relationship, even though they are seriously dating. The 'exclusive' terminology ensures that the couple knows they are devoted to one another only. The connection is a deep friendship, with some intimacy and the occasional date night. It might not be a full-fledged relationship, but to a degree, it is a relationship.

## BOYFRIEND OR GIRLFRIEND

Some people are uncomfortable with the title of boyfriend or girlfriend. They are usually the same folks who do not use the dating word. Some acknowledgement of how you plan to refer to yourselves is helpful. Casually dating someone does not mean you are necessarily the boyfriend or girlfriend. If you are exclusively dating someone however, then you are a boyfriend or girlfriend. Clarify this title with one another to make sure there are no surprises. There are many who are unsure what their connection is. Therefore, they continue dating other people or chatting them up. When people are hitting on you or asking you out, your immediate response should be, *"Thank you, but I'm seeing someone. I have a (boyfriend), (girlfriend)."*

## RELATIONSHIP

A relationship is where you are committed to the person you have been exclusively dating for some time. Exclusively dating someone is a commitment, but a relationship is taking it to a higher level. You might still be using the boyfriend or girlfriend title on occasion, but you are in a full-fledged relationship as well. This means you have both acknowledged that you are in a relationship with one another. You have gone through the dating process with them and have come to the realization that this is someone you trust, love and want to share your life with at this point. This is not to say that you are not experiencing those feelings when you are exclusively dating someone, but a relationship is an entirely different ballgame. It is a beautiful moment and yet at the same time, it will take work to keep it afloat. The Romance Angels know that the work has only just begun when a real relationship starts. They are present for those who request their assistance while in a relationship. In a sense, it is like buying a house to a degree. You have to take care of that house, work on it, and keep it up. The same goes for your relationship.

A couple who is mature and responsible about forging on in a relationship knows the value and benefit of coming together in an even more committed way. They understand that it is a perfected dance. You understand each other's quirks and know how they operate.

If you do not communicate, then your relationship will disintegrate. This means opening up and discussing everything including the serious matters. You are partners and a team who have made a pact to forge on in life fighting the same cause together. You work through difficulties the way you might work with someone at your job in finding a solution to issues that arise. It is to know that you will have to compromise especially when your ego wants to do what it wants YOU to do. This is not living in the Light, but in selfishness. When you are selfish, self-centered and act out in your own interests, then you create bad Karma. This Karma grows when the particular choices you make negatively affect another human soul. This can include leaving a relationship to feed your ego. It is different when you leave an abusive relationship or that person has been engaging in intimate acts with other people. Even talking intimately with another person while you are involved with someone else is an emotional betrayal.

You might be riding sky high after you make a selfish move that affects the one you left, but the initial selfish act you participated in grows and suddenly things start going wrong in your life. Most human souls do not realize that it is their Karma. When you are selfish, how would you know you acted selfishly? You are too self absorbed and narcissistic to care. Human souls have relationships throughout the course of their Earthly life in order to gain specific knowledge pertaining to their soul's agreement. No one is exempt from this regardless if one does not have at least one serious relationship in their life.

In a serious relationship, the couple usually tends to have their eye on living together at some point. There are many successful relationships where the couple has separate residences. In those cases, they are spending quite a bit of time practically living at each other's places. They might as well live together.

Relationships can also be anyone that your soul connects with for any length of time. This can be for a few minutes or a few decades. It can be your love relationship mate, your boss, colleague, a friend or even neighbor. It can be someone you have met in an airport terminal holed up together for a two-hour delay. You share a conversation that enlightens or prompts you to make a positive change within you. They might have connected with you to deliver specific information that ends up assisting you with something more pressing in your life.

When you merge into an actual love relationship, you have likely experienced some ups and downs with that person during the dating stages. You know how to navigate effectively with each other when there is a disagreement. When you were exclusively dating, you might not have shared every moment or your whereabouts, however in a relationship, it is a mutual alliance. You will be receiving questions that you might not have had before. "I saw you talking to that girl. What was that about?" How about, "Can you accompany me to this work thing?"

In a relationship, you are already aware that your mate may need extra reassurance that you are with them from time to time. You know how your mate is and will not be exactly like you. Perhaps they need additional emotional support or physical affection. Maybe they crave heavy doses of romance or they prefer not to have the hearts and flowers kind of love. These are situations where the couple does these things for their partner, because they care about them. It might not be what they are typically into, but this is where compromise comes into play. You gain knowledge in the relationship such as opening up or revealing your heart more. You are here on this planet for love after all. Do you really think it's to work a 9-6 job for the duration of your Earth life? Sure, you need to make money to survive, but that's not why you are here. It is to learn to love and exude love.

It is awesome to be an enterprising person in business,

and to strive for financial success that ensures the stability and security your human needs crave. However, you do not want it to take over your life to the point where you ignore your mate indefinitely. There will be times where you might have a busy period at work. It is another thing to allow it to consume and rule your entire Earthly life. The Romance Angels stress on the need for you to balance both your work and your home life. Doing this ensures that you are in a happier state of mind while attracting in the abundance your human soul desires.

By the time you are in a relationship with this person, you already know them pretty well. This means you know what some of their faults and moods are like. You know how they are, what makes them tick, or what upsets them. You need to be at a place of being open with that other person when you cross over into the 'in a relationship' territory. At that point, you may have already discussed if you will one day live together and what kind of places or cities you would like to live in. You discover if it is in harmony with the other person during the dating phase. You know if they want kids, or a family, or pets, etc.

How is your partner with children, animals or their own family? These are clues to what they might be like when you are living with them. When you are living with someone in a relationship, you are with this person day in and day out. Is this something your ego will be able to handle? It is certainly important that the partnership have their separate lives and hobbies to an extent. If you are with the same person every second, then you will be driven crazy. Human souls need space and independence every now and then. This helps them realign and reassess their goals, visions and thoughts. Successful couples are in constant communication with one another even if they are on a sabbatical alone while the other is teaching a class in another city. Many households have couples where both of them work all day. When they arrive at home at the end of the day, they may have personal activities to attend to. Maybe one of them enjoys swimming at the gym after work on Wednesday's while another meets his buddies on the field for a baseball sport. Healthy relationships welcome the separate, but equal lives they have together. This ensures the longevity while keeping it all balanced.

You are each other's friend and confidante. Having your own life is beneficial pending that you do not neglect your partner. Some long-term successful couples have protested that the passion or the sex has waned at times while together. Passion and sex in a relationship is a helpful component, but it is normal for happy committed couples to reach a place of no sex or a drought. When this happens, you must talk about it with one another. Take it seriously by finding ways to unleash the passions within you both. This should not be too difficult because all of the other positive components that keep you together already exist. This is why you are together to begin with. When you have the other positive qualities in the relationship such as a great friendship, companionship, communication, trust and enjoyment together, then it is relatively easy to move it into a sexual way.

Growing subconscious fears contribute to lack of sex in a relationship. Some couples become too comfortable with each other where it feels like you are roommates or siblings. This does not mean your relationship is over. On the contrary, this is where you put those working on the relationship skills to good use. Find ways to re-ignite that exciting passion between you both. I have a strong sexual drive by nature, but I am also very patient with someone I love when it comes to that. You may need to put in some effort and not be afraid to talk sexually with your partner. Send them little sexual texts and emails or start complimenting them and their body. Your partner should be open and receptive to this. Drop your guard and those pointless walls built around you and let loose with each other. Come up with some sexual exercises that you can both work on together. Develop self-love for your own body and your lovers' body. If you do not love yourself, then how can you love someone else?  Take romantic trips with one another and put together candle light dinners.  Hold hands more.  Cuddle.  Hug.  Get into it and put in some effort!

You should never jump to move in with someone in a relationship right away.  Wait until the honeymoon blush has worn off.  This is about the 18-month mark after you first met or started dating.  If they have lasted that long with you, then you know there is a great shot at making the living together part work.  There is no set time on when you have to move in, as there are couples that have been in relationships with each other for years, but choose not to live together nor have immediate plans to.  Exceptions always exist such as an older couple who comes together and gets married within the same year.  They have the maturity level to ensure it lasts.  They don't have the excessive hang ups that come with someone who is younger.

There is no such thing as an open relationship despite the modern day world pushing for that title.  Open relationships are essentially, *'friends with benefits'*.  This is what it should be labeled.  There are swinger couples that live with one person in a relationship, but might be unsatisfied sexually with that person.  They prefer to invite another person into the bedroom on occasion.  They are more into sex and agree on living together for companionship, while bringing in additional partners for sexual enjoyment.  This is a mutually reciprocated agreement between them.

## Marriage, Civil Union, Commitment

Marriage, civil union, or a commitment ceremony is the next step after relationship.  You have been in a relationship with the same person for years and you are both happy with it.  You may both choose to make it even more official.  This is where you are taking a big step in joining in a marriage under the eyes of human law.  This includes all the tax benefits that it entails. This also includes the dangers if you decide to divorce. It can be taxing financially and emotionally if you are both not in sync when you decide to dissolve the marriage. Marriage is not always a romantic circumstance, although it can be. It is a business alliance as if you are starting your own business with a partner. This partner is your soul mate and they are on the same page with you. You both already know quite a bit about the other person and you function well as a team. You are each other's family through all good things and bad. Only marry when you have no problem knowing there is no out. You know there will be lows as well as great highs and you are still okay with that. You will work together to fix it as if it were your business. You would not walk away from your business immediately if there were problems, would you? You would find ways to fix it.

Another label for marriage can be a civil union or some choose to conduct an official ceremony even if the government does not recognize it. This might be the case with Same Sex couples in certain states or countries. The bottom line is that it does not matter what the law, government or other people think about your relationship. It only matters what you and your partner choose to call it. You may choose to say you are married, even if you did not go to a government facility to have it documented under the eyes of the law. Some couples like to have a special spiritual ceremony whether it is personal between them, or an all out wedding with all the trimmings and guests. This is in keeping with the fun and joy that a love relationship is. Love is a celebration!

# Chapter Ten

## Random Messages From Spirit

    Guides and Angels do not always divulge ALL information on what's to come for each individual. Some of the reasons are that you need to have certain life lessons and experiences on your own before you are shown the next great step. You need to be content with where you are at before the good stuff comes in. Some souls can take years before they get comfortable with that if at all. Come to the realization that it is best to be grateful for what you have now. Complaining or being upset about it doesn't do you, your body, or soul any good. I've witnessed others live in that perpetual state of unhappiness indefinitely wondering why no miracle has come about. The odds are that these mini-miracles have been brought to them, but they were too over-involved in despondence to notice. I've certainly been there myself, but I've noticed that the moments where I am completely content and not fixated on the future, then the great career position comes about or the next love relationship enters my life.

## Power of Prayer

Ask and you shall receive. Pray about the changes you'd like to see happen in your life. Have faith and believe in it. Focus only on what you desire to see happen and not what you don't want. For example say something like, "Please guide me to friendships with like minded interests." Also add in, "Thank you."

Be grateful for what you have. "Thank you for keeping my body healthy in all ways. I'm grateful that I have shelter, etc."

Shifting your outlook can take practice and time, but before you know it, you will start noticing the positive changes happening in your life. Ask Archangel Michael to surround you with white light protecting you from lower energies when you pray. Praying for others has therapeutic effects. When you send positive words about someone else whether in the form of a prayer, affirmation or a statement, you are raising your soul's energy vibration. This process not only results in additional healing light sent to the other person, but this same light is magnified and re-directed back onto yourself as well. This only solidifies the theory that your thoughts do produce things, whether those thoughts are of yourself or someone else. When someone upsets you and you find yourself complaining about them, you are not only sending negative energy to that person, but that energy you're toying with acts as a mirror reflecting the same energy right back onto your soul. This is why it is important to catch yourself when you discover that you are spending more time using negative words about a situation and quickly modify them to be optimistic. Sending prayers or positive words to someone else is a win-win situation because it not only has the added benefit of elevating the other person's soul, but it also improves yours.

Sending positive prayers and affirmations to others will help as much as the other person allows it to. They have free will choice to go against the prayers and override any heavenly assistance offered. If they are choosing to stay in a negative space, or they're making choices that their ego insists on, then there is little you or Heaven can do. When you send prayers for another person, the angels will continue to uplift that persons thoughts and nudge them in the right direction continuously hoping that person will notice.

Sometimes you pray for change with little to no instant results. When you notice that nothing has happened, your ego kicks in and causes you to worry. The ego wants things immediately. You start to lose faith when you notice nothing has changed. Your unanswered prayers sometimes have other factors that need to come into play first before you notice changes.

There are times when your prayers are answered. The way it is answered might not be in the manner you expect it. You fail to notice the blessings that have indeed trickled into your life. There are the repeated signs you ignore that your Spirit team is asking you to do. It could be something as simple as signing up to take a particular class or go to a seminar. They put the signs in front of you. You continue to notice the same seminar flyer, but you never act on it or equate it to Divine orchestration. Sometimes your Spirit team has to maneuver certain pieces of the puzzle before you notice the changes. Other times they want you to endure a particular experience as part of your karmic thread, life lesson and growth. The insight you gain in what appears to be a less than stellar situation carries over into your new situation. You have the revelation of why the experience was necessary. "Oh, I see why it didn't happen right away." It all eventually makes sense.

## A Prayer

*"I'd like to thank God for creating this planet and its entire habitat, plants, wildlife, animals and the beauty of all of the nature surroundings. Help me to take care of it and never take it for granted. Thank you for providing me with all of the necessities I need to survive in a human body such as food, clothing, housing and money. Help me to align perfectly with my higher self and its purpose while here. Thank you for assisting me to always express love."*

## THE EGO'S WRATH

The ego is what convinces you that you are not qualified. It delays you from moving forward with your life purpose. It prompts you to experience any negative emotions such as jealousy, stress, sadness or hatred. The ego is your lower self, which is not of God. It is the part of you, which acts childish and immature or causes drama. Frustrated and fearful human souls might join in a gang or cult. It covers up what they feel is lacking with a false confidence. It is also a learned trait. A human soul does not enter this life desiring to enter into a cult or gang. When you think for yourself, you do not have any interest in latching onto others to form a gang or group. Do not allow your ego or anyone else's for that matter to convince you that you are not qualified or not ready for something. You were born ready and qualified. Ignore the negative voices that attempt to sabotage you. Go after what you want and do not allow doubt or reservation to enter the equation

Human souls must live with one another and learn how to love. You learn how to love when you accept that others are not like you. They do not live the way you do. Outsiders who have different interests and lifestyle choices than you will enter your vicinity. Your vicinity is your community, city, workplace, or on any level. Do you welcome them with open arms or are you immediately suspicious? Accepting someone with love is having an understanding that different people live in this world with varying belief systems and this is okay. This does not mean you must accept and love someone who is harmful, gossipy, and violent towards others. Accept and love those who have a different way of living than you without judgment. This includes those who have varying religious or political beliefs. This also includes those who are of a different nationality or sexual orientation than yours. If someone is acting out from their ego with these types of circumstances, then pray for them and walk away. I realize this can be easier said than done, but I'm sure you've noticed when you have been equally judgmental towards them that you've experienced an uncomfortable feeling inside.

A greed mentality exists in every part of the globe. One example would be the kind that plagues America. One of the biggest shopping days of the year in the United States is called "Black Friday". This takes place the day after the Thanksgiving holiday every November. It is a day when material items are marked down to a great degree. It is only a handful of products which are marked down for a specific time limit. They are mostly products you do not really need. This leaves many fighting over material items. If you do an internet search on the crimes and violence broken out on Black Friday, you would be amazed. Thanksgiving is a holiday that has more or less forced most of America to head to their family's house to break bread and cook a turkey. The meaning of the long weekend has lost its flavor. It's now all about shopping. It's about Black Friday and now Black Thursday. More retail stores are opening in the late evening on Thanksgiving Day. This is of course a backwards step for humanity, where human priorities are dominated by greed. Close up shop. Take a break. Chill out and relax!

This is anyone and everyone that is participating in Black Friday on Thanksgiving. The exception is the employees who are expected to work.

I've always found Thanksgiving to be an odd holiday.

This is especially when you dive into the history of how the holiday started to begin with. Human ego started a war on another culture of people in order to take over the land. On the flipside, I'll accept a holiday that does its best to bring people together. This is the point of Thanksgiving in current modern times. There will never be enough of bringing people together going on. What is unfortunate is that a holiday needs to happen in order for this to be accomplished. This should be all year round.

When I connected to my Spirit team for messages for Thanksgiving and Black Friday weekend, surprisingly the first thing that came up was LOVE. Love is the biggest feeling experienced when you cross over. It is Heaven and the spirit world's mantra. Love. Joy is right up there with love. Remember what is ultimately important to your soul and why you are here. It is to love. It is to give and to spread love. This mantra should be adopted everyday and every minute of your life. When all else fails, remember: LOVE. Think and breathe the word always. Be grateful. Be thankful and above all....love. When that fails, love again, and repeat.

One of the strengths that everyone has in common is the capacity to operate purely from a place of love. Everyone was born with this gift. Negativity, stress, emotional instabilities are all learned traits. Love is what you are made of and what you were born with. It is the only place you can find true power and strength.

Anyone can connect to Spirit who works at it. You have to take care of yourself on all levels, such as physically, spiritually, mentally and emotionally. When you have raised your vibration on those key well-being traits, then the closer you are to receiving accurate, mind-blowing, heavenly communication.

We are all on the precipice of a new energy. Heaven has sent millions of souls to enter this world to usher in this change and set the example in a myriad of ways. The spirit world has been sending souls to enter into human form throughout history to enact particular changes that progress

God's Earth. These same human souls were crucified. They were people from Jesus Christ to those who were accused of witchcraft. They are and were those who had views that were out of this world. The new group of what some refer to as Light workers, Indigos, Crystals, Rainbows and many others has increased with great magnitude after the 1960's. More of them were rushed in through the 1970's and even more into the 1980's, 1990's and beyond.

## SHIELDING

Because of the harsh energies plaguing the world in other people, it is important to shield yourself and your soul. Shielding is the act of calling in your Guide or Angel and asking them to shield you with protective white light. If I happen to run into someone with a bad mood, I call in Archangel Michael immediately and ask him to shield me from their energy, while extricating them from my vicinity as well. In the past, I would've let the person's mood affect me or I would take responsibility for their upset. Those days eventually became long over to the point where I was a completely different person then.

Be careful not to over shield either yourself or your business. Sometimes you might surround yourself with so much protective light that you are invisible. No one can see you or your business. Ask that the light heaven sends down to shield you be permeable. This means that only the love enters the shield.

If you do not have deep clairvoyance, then you might not see all of the lights that are around you and every living thing, person, organism or plant. The lights can be seen from Heaven, but not necessarily for the average human soul who tends to block that connection and ability. The exception is someone with a strong clairvoyance channel.

Shield yourself when reading media stories. Most of it is

toxic drama that the media puts in front of the masses on a minute-by-minute basis anyway. The planet is enveloped in a thick tar of dark debris that lowers vibrations and causes a massive array of health issues in the process. Be aware of what is going on in the world to an extent, but do not get buried underneath all of it.

It does seem to be in your face whenever you turn your head. When I'm not in front of the computer, I'm in the dark to what's going on in the world. This is of course unless a friend mentions something major going on that I had not heard of. I do not watch television, but when you log into your email account for example the headline ticker is splattered all over it. It might be on your friends social networking wall thread when you log into that. The great thing about my official social media group account is that I can choose what high vibrational accounts I like or follow, so all I see on my wall are those posts. On my personal social media account for example, they are filled with friends or acquaintances who sometimes post things that are more gossip, negative or toxic worthy. I skim over it quickly, although it is rare with my bunch to begin with, but it's still there at times. Using your social networking account to vent or express negative feelings on a regular basis sends this energy to others and back onto yourself.

I shut that down years ago and do not hang around it. Those who know me personally know my deal and how I operate. It is rare that I see drama brought up with me. It does happen once in awhile, but others can sense I am not interested as I have a good measure of apathy and detachment. I might say something along the lines of helping someone, and then continue on my way, rather than assisting in pro-longing the drama. I am in and out, and away quickly in those situations.

I am outside and in the car and travelling through highly tense areas with wall-to-wall cars. You have stressed out drivers on the edge. This is where one can be most affected because you cannot escape it, unless you move to a quiet country and nature like setting with little to no people. This is why it is important to shield before you hit the road. This is so that you are not absorbing all of that wasted energy darted in your direction. When you absorb this energy it weighs you down, jars with your emotional state, and makes you feel tired and irritable. A friend once suggested smiling and waving to tense drivers or people walking by. Notice their face warm up and relax. Kill them with love and kindness! Put in an extra effort to spread love.

## Cord Cutting

Whenever you come into contact with a friend, family member or love relationship, you form a cord to them. This cord looks much like a gasoline hose to a clairvoyant. The hose is hooked onto you and this other person. If the person you have a cord attached to is moody, angry or showcasing other negative emotions, then this will harden the cord and cause you to absorb that energy from them. If a loved one has crossed over to the other side, your cords are still connected. This is the case if you had a strong tie on Earth. These are energetic cords and both departed spirits and human souls share this same energy. Cord attachments are not always negative, but they can be. You would know if the cord has turned dirty. You feel weighted down or lethargic when you think of that person. You feel negative thoughts or anxiety when that person is on your mind. This means you need to cut the cords with that person, especially if it is preventing you from functioning or moving forward.

Cord cutting is where an angel or spirit being cuts the etheric cords of attachment that form on your soul. Archangel Michael is the go to Archangel for cutting cords. There is no difference whether the person is on the Earth plane or in the spirit world. It is an etheric cord connecting two souls. Your soul can have hundreds of cords attached to it, as there is no limit. However, it is unlikely one would have that many at one particular time, because you would feel it and know it. Your mind is not thinking of hundreds of people at once. If someone has not been on your radar for some time, meaning you have had no communication for years, then it is not likely you would have a cord attached to that person.

These cords attached to someone else can be communication devices with that person. This is why married or committed couples for example know and sense what is going on with their partner without them uttering a word. The same goes for exes. Yes, I have communicated with exes telepathically on occasion in the past. This was long before I controlled my thoughts. This communicating with them telepathically prompted them to reach out to me, which depending on the ex is not always a good thing. Call on Archangel Michael to cut those cords daily. I go into more detail about Shielding and Cord Cutting in my book, *"Warrior of Light: Messages from my Guides and Angels."*

## TAKE CARE OF YOUR BODY

Some of the many messages from the other side are repetitive. The reason is they want everyone working at optimum levels. This is not for their benefit, but for yours. They know you will be happier and more at peace when you are radiating high vibrational energy. There are times when I have had to struggle to remember adhering to some of their wisdom. As disciplined as I am, I still have a human ego that gets in my own way once in awhile. No one is perfect and nor is Heaven expecting or asking for perfection. They do however know what your soul desires. They know what steps will help you get there. You do the best you can. The more passion and dedication you have to make positive improvements in your life, then the closer you will be to achieving abundance. Exercise is a key factor in whipping your entire state of mind, body and soul into shape. Your soul feels weighted down when your body is not functioning at optimum levels. This happens when you do not take care of it. Be sure to get regular bouts of exercise for at least fifteen minutes a day. The more the better, but starting low and working your way up is an easy way to make the transition. Turn on your music player and get into it. Music raises your vibration and uplifts your spirit closer to God so crank it up! Eating fresh fruit and vegetables are another of the many ways to raise your vibration. Make the pact to care about your body and soul.

Juicing some of your fruits and vegetables helps the nutrients absorb into your body much more readily. Juicing contributes to keeping your body in shape, while cleansing your organs and adding increased energy levels. This gives you more power and energy during the day to put towards being productive. You have more quality time to spend with friends and family or any other healthy pursuits. This is instead of crashing early unable to gather enough strength and energy for those additional luxuries. This is a positive contributor to your long-term happiness and success. I bought a juicer in 1999 for less than $100. Fifteen years later I was still using the same juicer, so I definitely got my money's worth.

A shot of Blue Green Algae and a shot of Wheatgrass does a body good. Wheatgrass is a superior detoxifier that contains Chlorophyll. Chlorophyll is a great blood builder. It purifies the liver and decomposes free radicals in the body. This also slows down the aging process. Wheatgrass has many benefits that rid your body of unfriendly bacteria. Chlorophyll also comes in capsule, tablet and powder form. Blue Green Algae is high in nutrients and is a natural energy booster. It contains a high concentration of powerful antioxidants that strengthen the immune system. It also stimulates and aids in the regeneration of damaged body tissues. It also reduces depression symptoms prompting you to be more able to cope with everyday stress. The benefits and effects are evident after regular use.

It is vital that you get at least fifteen to thirty minutes of cardio exercise a day. This can include brisk walking, jogging, biking, running or hiking. Although going for a stroll after a meal is relaxing and allows your body to absorb the fresh air outdoors, this does not meet the daily exercise requirement. Physical activity is important for a myriad of reasons. It raises your vibration so that you can hear the messages and guidance from Heaven more readily. It strengthens your body enabling it to fight off potential illnesses or diseases. It gives you a clear mind and joyful state. All of this attracts in positive circumstances and great luck your way.

## Dancing and Singing

Dancing raises your vibration! So get up, move and hit the dance floor! This is a quick way to awaken all of your cells at once. Dancing prompts you to feel alive. It opens your aura and soul right up. Your inner light blasts wide open and radiates when you dance. It does not matter where you do it. Take some time to crank up your stereo at home. Dance in your living room or in your bedroom. Sway your body and get into it. Do not feel ashamed. The spirit world is bathed in the fun of singing and dancing for a reason. They do not place the kinds of shameful or embarrassing burdens on their backs the way a human soul's ego might.

When you dance you experience joy, gratitude and optimism. Some of our greatest entertainers throughout the world's history whose specialties have been dancing on stage or screen agreed to a human life to bring this wonder to the masses all at once. Their goal is and has been to liven up human souls who get stuck in the mundane unable to break loose. It took a long time for human souls to become aware of the joys of singing and dancing. The spirit world agreed to send souls to enter into human form and display what they have been doing on all spirit planes for eons. And that is dancing and singing! Your thoughts and feelings are uplifted when you dance. Who cares if you feel you have two left feet and are tone deaf. To God, you are perfect in every way, so do it anyway! This is for your own long-term health benefit.

Society has established so many ridiculous rules that hold human souls captive. This includes restricting each other from opening up and releasing. There was once a bigger stigma with dancing when it came to men specifically. Men were trained by society to remain withdrawn, the rock, unemotional, yet strong. Men were trained to not display emotion or feelings, let alone dance. To do so would make you weak. It's the opposite in fact. It takes strength to reveal feelings and emotion. Expressing yourself through dancing and singing releases your soul from the trappings of human life!

Statistics have shown that women live longer than men. Why do you think that is? For one, women tend to be more expressive with their emotions and feelings. They do not typically hold this stuff in. They are receptive and nurturing by nature. However, a shift has taken place over the last few decades where the life expectancy for both men and women are relatively similar. This is due to men being taught to be more open, feeling oriented and expressive. They get out there on the dance floor and do not care what others think. They're not afraid to move to the music. In fact, even though there are still some traces of stigma in certain areas around the world with dancing, the newer souls coming into this world now are defying those absurd stereotypes that once held the human soul prisoner. European cultures such as Italy or Spain tend to radiate their love for dancing and expressing joy full time. Other cultures are slowly moving in that direction in a bigger way. Let's crack it wide open!

Dancing and singing releases those rigid blocks that later cause health concerns. You live a longer more prosperous life when you get into the groove.

One interesting dichotomy my Spirit team has shown me is that some partake in drugs or drinking tons of alcohol and then they get out on the dance floor. The reason this is contradictory is that even though they are at the clubs or a party dancing which raises their vibration, the alcohol and drugs soon drop your vibration to a great degree. It's counterproductive where your vibration is not rising at all.

There is nothing wrong with alcohol in moderation or that it is kept to a healthy minimum of two glasses, but the dancing and singing they're talking about is the natural kind when you're not on any mind altering substances. The dancing and singing is what will raise your vibration and overall view naturally without the need for a toxic substance. Alcohol releases inhibitions, but a human soul with a high vibration releases these inhibitions naturally without any harmful vices. Crank up your stereo or music player and move that body! Not only does your vibration rise, but these movements tone and strengthen your body with regular bouts of dancing exercise. Dancing and singing raises your vibration and releases your higher soul from its body confinement. This prompts your entire aura to feel alive!

# HALLOWEEN

Halloween is one of the more popular holidays celebrated on October 31st. Nowadays it is mostly a time where people have fun with it by dressing up in costume, watching scary movies or visiting haunted houses and theme parks. There are myths and legends associated with the holiday, but most of it is not true according to my Spirit team. It is a day to remember the deceased. It ended up taking on an entirely new meaning over time. People started to associate the dead with ghosts and goblins. You can see how the holiday can easily take on a life of its own.

When I asked my Spirit team if the veil is thin between our world and their world, I received a surprising, 'yes'. The reason is mostly due to there being so much energy focused on the dead by human souls around Halloween time. Because this energy is so potent on the day of Halloween itself, this invites and attracts more of that energy in from the other side. Even though people are doing it just for play, it is having an effect. The effects are harmless to an extent, although you should shield your soul on Halloween or October 31st. Take precautions that you do not invite unwanted negative spirits into your vicinity who drain your energy. Those on the other side are pure, but there are spirits who are what some might describe as being in limbo. These souls refused to enter the light sometimes due to fear of what might exist such as judgment, etc. Instead, they attach themselves to human souls. They are usually attracted to darker lights and people bathed in addictions or in negativity in some manner. They coax that soul to continue on with the addiction or negativity.

The period around Halloween is actually a time of "transition" and "abundance". This is right on par with being about mid-way through the Fall or Autumn harvest in the Northern Hemisphere. My Spirit team did not get into the whole Halloween thing, but focused on using the Halloween energy to manifest abundance. Sow the seeds of what you want in your mind. It is a very powerful time including on All Saints' Day which falls right after Halloween on November 1st, as well as the Day of the Dead, which runs from October 31st through November 2nd typically.

# RAINBOWS

The Rainbow colors are a mixture of colors that different hierarchy spirits exude and radiate. They are high vibrational colors and lights. Archangel Raziel shows up wherever rainbows or rainbow colors are. There is nothing negative or cryptic about a rainbow connection. They are reflections of light created as a message from Heaven. They are one way that someone on the other side is sending you a message if you are seeing the same symbol repeatedly. Heaven will communicate through repeated symbols and signs that have the same pattern. It would depend on what type of help you are asking for if any to decode those symbols.

If your question or request for Heavenly assistance were in regards to a work promotion or something having to do with material success, the rainbow would be a sign that the pot of gold is coming up or good news. The rainbow can also be a bridge or a passage that things are looking up. It also means hope and assurance that God is indeed present. Of course whenever God is present it is always a reminder that you need to be exuding love more often. He is always present, but when He is showing signs of His bigger presence, then it would show up in many forms including rainbows. He does not reveal his presence through violent acts despite what some might believe. Those are the acts of human ego. God is all love.

## Twin Flame Love

You have many soul mates and only one twin flame. Most people do not connect with their twin flame in this lifetime. Twin flames are highly evolved souls. Since you are here for the sake of growing your soul, it is rare that you incarnate at the same time as your twin flame. Your twin flame is the other half of your soul. If your twin flame passes onto the other side long before you do, they will wait for you on the other side. They may choose to be one of your guides in order to work with your Spirit team to place potential soul mates in your path. They help you cope and strengthen your soul so that you can continue on the rest of your current Earth life. They do not want you to suffer or grieve over your temporary detachment from them, especially since they are alive and well. You have other important matters to attend to while you are here. Your twin flame does not want you distracted from that because they are in a different spiritual plane. You connect with your twin flame in this lifetime if you are on a higher spiritual path or you have evolved. Your twin flame would need to be in this same space as well or at least close to it. I go into more detail about both soul mates and twin flames, and how to recognize them in my book, *"Warrior of Light: Messages from my Guides and Angels."*

It's sometimes difficult for a human soul to comprehend or connect with their twin flame on the other side, even though they are without realizing it. To your twin flame from the spirit world, they're very connected to you more than you know. You will be with your twin flame soon enough. To them, your life is a blip that lasts one minute in the spirit world. You may feel the presence of your twin flame at times as they send love to your heart. Even if you are feeling love for a new soul mate in your life, your twin flame is playing a part in opening your heart up to that soul mate. Your twin flame can also be of the same gender as you. Twin flames are the deepest love relationships that last lifetime after lifetime.

Your soul does not always re-incarnate immediately if at all. The ones that typically incarnate are new souls and teacher souls. You and your twin flame choose the when or how you will incarnate on Earth together if it is intended to happen. You agreed to this particular design. You likely won't remember that now, but your memory is restored when you cross over. You will re-connect with your twin flame when you cross over if they are currently in the spirit world. They are one of the many souls that greet you as long as they're not already living an Earthly life at the time of your human death.

The souls that re-incarnate immediately are the ones that

had an Earthly run just to have an Earthly life with no other purpose than that. Human souls that commit suicide will generally re-incarnate sooner than later. This is because they cut their life short before they could fulfill their purpose. They need to go back and finish what they started. They move through an incubation process where their soul is restored before that happens. No soul is forced to live an Earth life. They make that choice with their Spirit team. They usually want to have an Earth life as they have more perspective while on the other side than they would on Earth. There is an importance in terms of their soul's growth on Earth that is understood. Other souls agree to incarnate in order to be a spiritual teacher on some level. The spirit world understands the significance of improving one's soul, other souls, and God's planet.

# Chapter Eleven

## MESSAGES FROM THE ARCHANGELS

In my book, *Warrior of Light: Messages from my Guides and Angels*, I dedicated a chapter to sixteen of the most popular Archangels titled, *Connecting with the Archangels*. It included some of the traits, specialties, stories, and how to work with these Archangels. There was great interest in the Archangels content from readers. This chapter surrounds some of the practical messages from the sixteen prominent Archangels. This is an addition to what is featured in the *Warrior of Light* book.

There are legions of Archangels that reside in many of the dimensions that exist. Archangels are God's arms and hands, therefore when you communicate with an Archangel, you are communicating with God. They raise your vibration in order to pick up the messages from God. Archangels are infinite and able to be everywhere at once. This is the same way God is everywhere at once. The Archangels are immensely powerful and tackle larger scale issues in all spirit planes and dimensions. They reside in a dimension higher than any spirit guide, angel, or departed human soul.

The Archangels are available to any soul who calls on them and requests their assistance. They are egoless and have no emotional interest in the mundane triviality that human souls fret over. They are unaffected by ego demands. They only see your natural state of being.

The following chapter contains practical messages and affirmations from some of the more popular and well-known Archangels. The messages all have the same goal, which is to assist you in shedding away circumstances, vices, and people that do not serve your higher purpose. Every Archangel has a wide array of specialties that they focus on. This chapter is the longest chapter in this book and contains some of the guidance that can assist you in day-to-day human matters. You can call upon any Archangel for intervention, guidance and assistance. This can be done mentally, out loud or even in writing. Saying something like this has invited assistance in, *"Archangel Michael, please help me with...."* For additional information about the Archangels specialties listed in this chapter, check out my book, *"Warrior of Light: Messages from my Guides and Angels"*, or the mini-book, *"Connecting with the Archangels"*.

# Messages from Archangel Michael

Archangel Michael is the Archangel to call on when you experience fear or apprehension. He can extract anyone out of your vicinity who is not operating from high integrity. If someone causes you uncomfortable feelings, then he will remove them at your request. He explains that some souls create self-induced fear that circumstances in their life are out of control. When the circumstance is examined from ones higher self or a detached point of view, it is apparent that the situation is unnecessarily hyped up to be bigger than it truly is. You witness this behavior in outlandish and dramatic human reaction by the masses to the latest media headline alone. The ego enjoys conjuring up unnecessary worry and drama. They will somehow come to the conclusion that an apocalypse is going to take place at any moment. There is never anything to fear when you have Archangel Michael by your side. Taking a step back you will notice the drama the mind creates is not based in reality.

The human souls that commit violent crimes attract in dark energies. These are souls who go against God and act on free will. They grew up heavily influenced by the people that raised them and the communities they grew up in. The human ego often goes mad from the nonsense of its surroundings. One half of the population is bathed in dark energy, while the other is in the light. The light has gradually been growing in numbers wiping out the darkness, but that does not mean it will not meet resistance. It helps to avoid anything and anyone that triggers negative feelings in you. This includes news sites filled with negativity and gossip. Human souls absorb that energy without realizing it. It seeps into your DNA, cells, and pores. Before you know it, you feel negative agitation that never lightens. Ask Archangel Michael to stand by your side and shield you with pink light so that only love can enter your aura. Follow his guidance to stay away from any and all drama around you.

Your thinking processes are the biggest culprit and cause of any unhappiness in your life. When you find you're moving into negativity, then adjust your thoughts into something more optimistic.

Do you feel like you are running around in a circle going nowhere? This is a clue that it is time to work on breaking away from the walls you have constructed around your soul. Find another path to go down that works. Break away from anything that is holding you back from moving forward. You may need to go back and re-examine what it is you want and how it is you are going about to obtain it. Look at what needs modifying in your life. Take that new-enlightened information and run with it. You will be that much closer to reaching fulfillment.

Avoid getting bogged down in a power struggle with your ego. Do not allow it to drown you in negative emotions. This is wasted energy that tests your patience. It causes one to react and jump into dangerous circumstances and choices without thinking. When the ego is upset, it causes unpredictable behavior in you, in others, and in your environment. There is a domino effect of energy which takes place from one over reactive human ego. Imagine thousands of people obsessively overreacting over the latest media story. They weigh in their two cents on the comment boards or on their social media pages spreading that plague like nobody's business. It is a waste of time since all drama works itself out in the end. It fades away and everyone forgets about it days later. They move onto the next biggest drama to fixate over. The ego blames everyone else, but themselves. This behavior goes on with some businesses, companies and even in the government. The public weighs in with their opinions and criticisms. All of that toxic energy is darted here, there and everywhere like bullets from an aimless gun. Stay away from the gossip and noise surrounding negative stories, as it will bury you in the dense energy pull on Earth. It is one thing to be aware of what is going on in the world, but another to absorb it all into your spirit. Sometimes when you experience negative emotions or turmoil, it attracts accidents and tumultuous circumstances in.

Ask Archangel Michael to protect you and shield you from all harsh situations. He can give you courage and confidence when you ask him to. He will help you to keep on going with whatever it is you are at odds with. If you feel weary from struggle, then Archangel Michael sends a reminder that you are more powerful than you give yourself credit for. With Michael by your side, you will persevere. Your ego wants to convince you that you cannot do anything and are incapable of success. These thoughts have no basis in reality. You can do it and have anything you choose. You have to fight for it and put in some effort. Sitting on your couch all day drinking beer will get you nowhere. Dive into the battlefield and claim what is yours.

Archangel Michael is also there for the Dad's as well. Many souls have naturally exuded a paternal role at some point in their lives to either their own children, or to those in the world just when that soul needed it most. Whether you are male, female, or a single parent is irrelevant. The role of a Maternal Father is a psychological one. Society has evolved where Father's used to be seen as distant and emotionless. They were seen as the primary breadwinner and the harsh disciplinarian. This did not quite work creating issues in how souls were developing. Positive creative emotional expression is the innate nature of souls. Inexpressiveness is a trait learned from the Father's of the past and at times with Mother's. This trait was ego taught and not God and spirit taught – since Heaven is all love.

The newer souls who chose to be born as male in this lifetime display both maternal and paternal traits. This is the same as souls born into this lifetime as female. Females are exuding masculine energy as well. This has stripped away what society has taught what a father should be. All souls when born share within them an equal amount of masculine and feminine traits as God intended. This creates more balance within your soul and ultimately in this world. Wear your masculine traits proudly regardless of your gender. Some have lost their Earthly paternal fathers, while other human souls had an abusive or absent father. They reached out to those who showed healthier father figure traits towards them. Anyone can be a father figure whether you are male or female. If you tend to be mostly receptive, then call on Archangel Michael to help balance that out with other masculine traits.

# Messages from Archangel Raphael

Archangel Raphael asks that you get out in the sunlight at least once a day when possible. He also demands that human souls get moving and exercise outdoors more often. The sun has positive benefits like reducing blood pressure and decreasing feelings of depression. A healthy balance of sunlight is more beneficial than getting none. It is not necessary to spend all day in the sun. Get out in the morning hours, or towards the end of the day when the sun is not beating down as harshly. Do this for at least fifteen minutes a day. Granted there will be seasons when the sun is virtually non-existent all day or it's unbearably cold or obscenely hot, but getting outside in the fresh air as much as possible is vital to your soul. In the cases where weather is extreme, it is understandable that precautions need to be adhered to. He's more pointing out to not make excuses to get outside when one is perfectly capable of doing so and the weather is fine.

Do you often feel drained and burned out? Are you overextending yourself? Many human souls sleepwalk through life going through the motions exhausted around the clock. This draining feeling causes you to wish you could just go back to bed and sleep until it is over. Call on Archangel Raphael to help in restoring your energy levels. He can help you get a restful night sleep and to awaken with natural energy.

Crimes have been committed regularly throughout history.

It seems particularly heightened these days because of the rapid way the media reports it across the Internet. It is in your face 24/7 with no hope for escape. This is still a Dark Age filled with many dark souls functioning in a human body. However, the Light has grown in many of the upcoming newer souls. This has brought the light in humanity to be equal to the Dark. Those living in the dark operate purely on ego and hostility. This is why the world is in terrible upset. If everyone was at peace, there would be no violent incidents, no hate, stress, or anger. What part are you playing in this equation to stop the madness? Are you a contributor to some degree on certain days? Are you teaching others about love, and to relax or to stop complaining? The more that others step in to correct certain poor behavior patterns in others, the closer to peace Earth will be.

Archangel Raphael can help energize you and increase your personal power. Sometimes you might have a day where there is an overload of information and feelings within you erupting to the surface. You may have to endure some ugliness or even delays on your life's path. When you gain enough wisdom from it, then the next guidance step is revealed to you. This step might take you in a different and brighter direction. This new road leads you towards enlightenment and a richer life.

Sometimes you experience loss, victimhood or antagonism. These are products of the ego and lower self. Even if you have felt pain or hurt, it is time to let that go and accept defeat. This way you can move forward to awesome pastures. Ask Archangel Raphael to help you let go of any pain you're hanging onto for dear life. Circumstances will look up when you let go of the control or outcome of how things will improve. The door opens to reveal something better when you release this tendency. Make your peace with whatever abuse or ill will might have happened to you by others and bring it to closure. See the lesson meant to learn or gain. Release it by moving on into the light of happier times ahead.

# Messages from Archangel Gabriel

Archangel Gabriel explains that your soul suffocates when you suppress your emotions and dreams. It is a volcano waiting to erupt and can no longer be contained within you. This is a sign that there is bountiful creativity you need to unleash through healthy sources such as taking on a hobby like painting, gardening, writing, photography or any other creative and artistic pursuit. Gabriel shows me a butterfly, which is a symbol of the great changes and shifts to look forward to when you unleash this creativity. This happens when you release any pent up non-action. Dig up those projects, ideas, and anything you have always wanted to do. Do not allow procrastination or negative self talk to stop you from diving into creative pursuits. If you have completed a project, then take it to the next level and market or sell it. Purchase some yellow flowers and place it close to where you typically hang out in your house. Yellow flowers awaken creative visions, intelligence as well as positive, new beginnings.

Gabriel pushes your soul to take immediate flight towards your goals, dreams and career. Whatever it is you have been procrastinating with, she will remove that ego delay tactic at your request. Archangel Gabriel is the Archangel who inspires and lights that fire within you to take action. She is the one that faces you in the direction of your dreams. She plants the seeds in your soul which ultimately gives birth to your creative pursuits. She pushes you out on stage where you belong!

Gabriel is all about creativity and passion. She will assist you with your creative endeavors, or even spice up your love life. This passionate spark can be the push you need to ask someone out on a date or take the relationship to the next level. Even if you have a spouse or love partner, she will light the passions within you to rekindle the heat for one another. Gabriel helps you express love in grand ways while adding the seductive charm to any courtship. She awakens all of your senses so that you experience deep gratification in all areas of your life. She will take your wildest ideas and push you to take action and turn the ideas into a reality. Archangel Gabriel is the muse to call on for all of your creative, artistic and passionate endeavors.

# Messages from Archangel Uriel

Do not lose sight of what is important on your journey here. It is easy to veer off track while functioning in a material based world on a regular basis. If you do not take just a little bit of time daily to detach from chaos, it can drown your spirit. Soon you find that days have passed and your thoughts have moved into words that are of a lower vibration. Uriel is the Archangel who focuses on improving your thoughts. He extracts the cobwebs that grow on absent minded words. He is also the one who infuses you with brilliant ideas as well as claircognizant hits of heavenly guidance.

Human souls have more power than they often realize. You have the power to manipulate energy in your surroundings and bring forth that which you desire with your thoughts. Do your best to work on keeping your thoughts and your words positive and high vibrational. It is understandable if you live in areas or with people that are predominately ego driven such as the big cities of the world. If you find yourself buried in negativity with no hope for escape, then this is a sign to give yourself a time out alone. Take a deep breath in, exhale, and relax. Call in Archangel Uriel to work with you in eliminating any low vibrational words you cannot get out of your mind. Ask him for intervention in modifying the negative sentences, complaints, or worry that your mind refuses to let go of. Shift your sentences to start with, "I love..." I love myself. I love who I am. I love that I have a car that runs. I love that I have a job that pays all my bills, and so forth. Modify your words to that of gratitude. If you find that you revert to negativity, then stop and re-word your sentences to more positive uplifting ones. It is work re-training your mind to get to that place of catching yourself every time you move into negativity. With practice you will get better at it. The results will be astounding in the end when you find that great things come your way. Your life is less stressful when you shift your thoughts into optimism.

Every thought that pops into your mind has an effect. This effect will determine whether you attract in what you want or what you do not want. Be careful of your daily thoughts, as you may not realize the power they have. You are always manifesting circumstances with the power of your mind, thoughts and visions. When your mind is plagued with worry, then guess what you are bringing into you? You're inviting in more of that negative stuff. This is why it is important that you catch yourself if you find that you are thinking negative thoughts. Quickly envision what you really want and ask that Uriel negate your harmful thoughts. Think about what you want as if it is already happening and you are living in that state. Even if what you want is not here yet, envision it as if you are happily living the life you want anyway.

Uriel works with those who daydream by allowing them to dream big. He pours wonderful ideas into these dreams. A child with an active imagination can create and attract beautiful circumstances over the course of their life. If that child has a hostile or naïve parent, peers or teachers, they may find the adult saying, "Stop daydreaming and get your head out of the clouds." This is unfortunate as that child could suddenly stop daydreaming. They will instead focus on doing what they feel is expected. When they grow up, they are not manifesting great things in their lives. This is due to the stigma that daydreaming is not taking action. On the contrary, daydreaming is where the seeds of your dreams begin. Our successful artists in history are proof of this. Daydreaming is the beginning stages of attracting in abundance. Abundance is where the necessities you need to live comfortably in life reside. As an adult, you might have a hard time keeping your thoughts positive. This is because society and your upbringing surroundings have taught you that daydreaming or living in the clouds will get you nowhere. Ignore that negative voice imprinted within the DNA of your mind. Daydream, live in the clouds, and envision what you want without human ego interference. Since your thoughts are producing things, you may as well think of what you want. Avoid wasting time thinking of the things you do not want. If you continue to think about what you don't want, then that is what you will get. Take control of your thoughts as if you're the driver of this car.

You cannot sugar coat any of the negativity that might happen around you. Nor can you turn your head away and pretend that everything is okay. When you read media reports of violent acts one after the other, it shines a huge spotlight on the ugliness that exists in the world. There is good and light, but unfortunately the media rarely reports the good stuff because those who run the media tend to function from ego. They feel reporting the good will be boring to people. Therefore they predominantly feed toxic, horror stories instead of balancing it with the good stuff. The media is ego driven and only interested in manipulation to make their quota. The human ego is under the influence and control of the media. The media does this successfully, since the human ego willingly follows. Ask Archangel Uriel to keep your thoughts focused on what matters most to your higher self and ignore the noise around you.

# Messages from Archangel Nathaniel

Archangel Nathaniel cuts people out of your life that no longer serve your higher self's purpose. This person they remove can be someone who is a constant energy sapper and yet you continue to keep them around. You do not owe anybody anything. You have to take care of you first. If someone is the cause of you feeling constant drain or burn out, then this may have detrimental effects on your health in the end. Not to mention it blocks abundance and delays you from achieving your goals. Nobody needs to live in stress. That way of life and thinking is over. Turn your back away from all of that and face the rays of God and Spirit flowing through you. Nathaniel helps you choose a better way to live by prompting you to move on and away from toxic people and choices. The connections have served their purpose. Do not think twice about it, but swim towards the light and leave those situations that are sitting in dark murky waters behind.

The planet Pluto is dark, cold, and icy. When negatively aspected, its energy causes wars, corruption and abuse of power. It also rips things out of your life without warning. It knows what is not working for you and eliminates it, yet it does this for a reason so that you can change, improve and grow. When you're hanging onto something toxic and it is removed with force, then this opens the door to bring in something even better. It is like the *"Tower"* card in the Tarot where it feels as if your structure is unfolding around you.

These experiences are happening for your higher good so that more improved circumstances can enter the picture. Good stuff has a difficult time entering your life when you cling desperately to the bad. The planet Pluto can feel like it is unleashing internal hell. It shines a light on the dark shadows of your needs and desires. It brings them out erratically in full view. It may cause you to act out and become unable to control your emotions over a specific issue. You grow to be hyper-focused on the issue giving it more power than it deserves. Archangel Nathaniel knows that your ego may throw a tantrum as he eradicates important people and toxic ways of living from your vicinity with force. He pays no mind to your upset, as he knows what will benefit your higher self in the end. Your ego desires and tantrums are irrelevant to him.

You might find that you become more vocal over areas in your life that you are unhappy with during this process. Nathaniel pushes you to do some deep examining of your psychological self. He yanks out the unpleasant parts of your personality for you to face. He prompts you to confront the dark sides of yourself and then forces you to deal with them in a big way. You have to do this in order to grow and wipe out any nonsense for good. This process will not remain upsetting since what precedes this will be followed by an immensely, beautiful, transformation. Purge anything and everything that no longer serves your higher self. Avoid getting buried in the intensity. The intensity you're faced with is your clue to what is going on in your life that needs serious addressing. This can be your own behavior, your unhappiness at a job, or a specific relationship with a friend or lover. If you do not address it, then Nathaniel will address it for you by removing what it is that you are holding onto as if your life depended on it.

An example might be if you lost your job unexpectedly. The immediate reaction might be devastation or depression. You might come to terms that it was a job you were never truly happy at to begin with and that it was likely a blessing in disguise. Still your ego does not take this ending lightly. It has a difficult time shaking it off wondering what's next. That is until you obtain another job that is even better and feels much like an answered prayer. You end up happier than you were beforehand. You come to the realization that the original crumbling of the previous job happened for a reason. Another example might be a relationship couple who has been at each other's throats for an unhealthy length of time, and that abruptly ends for good. Are you arguing with a friend and not seeing eye-to-eye? One or the both of you may have Nathaniel rip the friendship and connection apart. It is no longer serving a positive purpose on your higher path. These are some examples of how Archangel Nathaniel works with you. It may feel like you have no control over what and who is exiting your life. Know that there is a broader purpose for this transition. Patience and faith will be needed during that process.

# Messages from Archangel Jophiel

Archangel Jophiel is the Archangel who helps you clean house literally and metaphorically. She can help clear any clutter within and around your world. She will guide you to re-arrange your home so that it is conducive to your well-being. Living in a cluttered environment will cause all sorts of imbalances in your life. Jophiel nudges you to throw unnecessary items away or box them up. Human ego becomes attached to material items and necessities for a variety of reasons. It's understandable to have an emotional attachment to certain material items which have historical value for you. It is compulsive to save every little thing to which you have no use for. Pack rats are those who save every single item or piece of paperwork they're given. This blocks the flow of positive energy. You walk into an office or home that is piled sky high with unnecessary 'things' and you can feel the strangling energy. Call on Archangel Jophiel to help you function in a free flowing energy environment. She might guide you to remove files off your computer that you never use. You can move them to the trash, or transfer them to discs or flash drives, and store them away. She also helps you relax, calm down and take it easy. Cleaning up the clutter anywhere will uplift the energy prompting good things to come your way.

Jophiel might guide you to detox from technology. This is by disconnecting yourself from the Internet and television on occasion. Heaven always recommends that you avoid sensationalized headlines, gossip sites and time wasting activities online. When you feel as if you're having an 'off' day, give yourself permission to disconnect from it all. This will realign your soul with your body so that you can wake up the next day feeling refreshed and fantastic. When you ask for Archangel Jophiel's intervention, she will elevate your feelings and thoughts to the level of joy, which is the highest vibration. She will beautify you inside and out. This includes uplifting the energy in all of your surroundings including your car, home and office. Archangel Jophiel beautifies the land allowing the energy to flow. The trees, grass, flowers, plants and all of nature's preserves blossom into a glorious beauty. The same way that she does this with God's planet, she coaxes you to display your most magnificent self by pouring positive energy through your aura.

Archangel Jophiel says that all human souls must break free of negative fear energies. This energy grows when one is involved in gossip talk, or obsessing over the lives of celebrities, to the drama featured in media articles. These are time wasters, which delay you from your purpose.

Free your mind from the isolation of fear and misery. Get outside in nature in order to get unstuck. Break free from any self-imposed chains that have bound you and prevented you from moving forward. Have some healthy fun that raises your energy vibration. Fear or upset energy does nothing to help you or anyone. When you break down the reality of what is causing you to feel uncomfortable, you discover that your fears are not real. Everything works itself out when you invite a heavenly being into your life.

When Archangel Jophiel shows up, then a glimmer of hope is about to reveal itself to you. She wants you to be the star that your soul has always been. Human ego allows negative thinking patterns, such as doubt, to creep in and stall you from forward motion. She asks that you shun this mentality and allow your soul to shine bright with confidence. Be receptive to the blessings and good things handed to you.

She helps you think big and go after what you want without hesitation. You will get it!

Jophiel can also brighten up your relationships. She will help you ooze attractiveness to your partner. If you are looking to meet someone new, Jophiel will get you out there allowing your positive self to shine. Jophiel delivers the kind of cheery messages that circumstances are going to improve. She guides you to be brave and take risks in your endeavors. The universe cracks wide open ready to bless you with your desires when you are in a joyful state.

Dive right in to your dreams without waiting or second-guessing yourself. Make a list of what you want and take action steps towards each of them today. Keep the list handy in a small box and refer to it often to see what you can cross off your list once it has been conquered and achieved. This is what I do periodically. When I pull the list out at a later date, I have found that most of the things on the list could be crossed off.

Before you can bring in anything new into your life, you will need to clear out the outdated. Archangel Jophiel can help you release that which has been delaying you and holding you back from progress. You most likely already know what you need to let go of. It can be anything or anyone that brings you down or prompts you to experience inadequate feelings like depression, anger or stress. This also includes foods and substances that are not good for you. These substances cause your body to react negatively. When this happens you experience low energy or irritability. This delays you from taking positive action in your life and blocks the incoming flow of abundance.

Jophiel releases anything negative in your life so that you can be free to soar upwards where your higher self lives. She also focuses on the core chakras within your soul aura. These chakras govern all aspects of your life *(physical, mental, emotional)*. If a Chakra is dirty, then that creates an imbalance around that particular area of your life. When you release negative thoughts, patterns and people, then you are that much closer to obtaining your dreams.

Archangel Jophiel is surrounded by a rose light with tinges of yellow. She is the archangel who will drop rose petals in your path. She assists with things like pushing you to have a good time with an optimistic attitude, to putting together a function, party, festival or celebration. This is by beautifying everything she touches. If you find your absorbing negativity, then call on Archangel Jophiel and ask her to intervene and help you to remain positive and optimistic.

Jophiel brings people together including groups around the world with extreme viewpoints. She can help them find a common ground, but the trick is they have to ask for her help otherwise the friction will continue. She will assign specific warriors of light from these groups to instill them with some middle ground to connect and link everyone together.

She has talked about how the holidays that human souls have created lost its flavor. It has become all about shopping and spending frivolously. This rises during the Christmas and end of the year holidays. The United States is the biggest sufferer of this. She says they have lost sight of their true soul. It is all about gain, buying material things, and one upping someone else. People pack into malls, fighting traffic, parking spaces, pushing, and shoving each other just to buy a shirt. Stores are now staying open at unheard of hours, such as overnight on major holidays just to make another dollar.

What's important to focus on is your soul and why you are here on this Earthly plane. When you fall into superficiality, you lose sight of your purpose. You are here to love, to give love and to spread love. This mantra should be adopted everyday and every minute of your life. Deep down your soul knows what you can do to bring yourself back. Know your light, know your power, and know what you were born here to be. Love is who you are. Love is the source of all that you wish. Love is the source of power. The more that you love, the safer you are. The more that you allow yourself to love, the more powerful you are. All of your goals are to unite as many people as possible in peace, love and joy. When all else fails, remember: LOVE. Think and breathe the word always. Call on Archangel Jophiel to uplift your soul to this beautiful state.  If you feel agitation, then take immediate soul enhancement steps.  Head immediately to your nearest nature locale where there is little to no people.  Breathe in all of that beautiful nature, the trees, grass, flowers, and ask God and Archangel Jophiel to surround you with angels creating a healing love cushion.  Ask her to extract any negative ions that have latched onto your loving spirit.

# Messages from Archangel Raziel

You are creating the reality you want with every choice you make. This is done with the power of your thoughts and mood. Watch your thoughts and make sure that they do not shift towards something negative. You will manifest the energy that pervades your thoughts. Archangel Raziel encourages all souls to be an individual and not follow the herd. Everyone has unique gifts to utilize to their advantage while here. You were born with it and therefore can easily access it. Do not allow your innate talents to go to waste due to doubts, procrastination or fear. Raziel helps you become one with the entire Universe. When you are one with the Universe, you connect energetically to a higher frequency. Positive manifestation is what spawns out of this. Because you have the power to create your own reality, you also have the power to shift the bad stuff into something good. With Raziel by your side, you can magically conjure up the life you want by envisioning it with him and painting the picture in your mind. He can train you to learn how to keep it there. He also acts as a great publicist coaxing the real you to the forefront and marketing it to the masses. He can help promote your higher self's face, your work or career to others. This naturally draws in financial abundance.

A lizard has the ability to act as a chameleon shaping and shifting itself into nature. The same concept applies to you when you work with Raziel. You can be whoever it is you want to be. He says you already have the tools and capabilities to conquer whatever you desire. He warns you not to sway from this god-given gift and use it without guilt. Do not fall into negative self-talk or the imposter self that makes excuses so that you avoid bringing in the greatness you want. The gifts bestowed upon you are all encouraging and to be used in a positive manner. Raziel can also help you manifest great relationships by showering you with a magic that makes you magnetic to others. Envision the kind of love partner you want with Raziel. He will assist you in attracting that mate in. He advises you to be careful what you wish for, as you just might get it!

# Messages from Archangel Ariel

Archangel Ariel brings in messages of strength and courage. This has to do with your inner spirit and that you can accomplish anything you want to do. Ariel conveys this strength in her presence. The Lion travelling with her is a symbol of the ego, while Archangel Ariel is a symbol of the higher self. She has complete control over the lion. She is relaxed in holding the reigns of this wild beast. There is no struggle between her and the animal as they are both one. Ariel does not push against any resistance, but rather glides through it effortlessly. She does not fight the animal aggressively, but is assertive in her stance.

Archangel Ariel is immersed in radiant violet and purple colors. The colors are a symbol of magical manifestations and serenity. It invokes heavenly spirit and raises ones spiritual vision and consciousness.

Ariel urges you to tame yourself if you have been on a recent kick of lashing out in outbursts, negativity and upset. She warns you not to act or react impulsively, but rather systematically with bravery and self-control. Let go of the need to control things that get in your way. Refrain from taking other people's egos personally.

Ariel can also bring you positive new beginnings where finances and career related endeavors are concerned. Envision with her what it is you want as if it is already here. Remain upbeat, positive and hopeful about what is to come.

Do not allow any negative thoughts to take over. Ariel can bring in an increase in abundance and finances. Gifts may not be monetary based, but can be an improved relationship, or stronger commitment with your partner, or sense of self. It can be a long lasting spiritual joyful feeling. Call upon Archangel Ariel to work with you in creating this firm foundation where you can begin building the life you want upwards. She helps you to believe that you deserve it.

Retreat into a nature setting and call in Archangel Ariel and absorb in her powerful energy. Literally stop to smell the flowers as you take your time strolling through nature. Lean in to breathe in the flowers, plants, and all of nature. Hug a tree or sit up against it to release heavy toxic emotions. Nature is where spirits power is heavy. Take it all in allowing it to awaken and open your mind and senses. Take a deep breathe in and on the exhale release any lower vibrational thoughts and words. Nature affects all souls positively on a biological level. Flowers can brighten up a room, but they also raise your vibration. The different colors of a flower send particular messages to your brain pertaining to the flowers specialty. For example, green flowers can calm someone who is full of anxiety. Yellow flowers can brighten and uplift. Red flowers can awaken your inner passions and invite love into your life.

Ariel governs the changing of the seasons. The seasons changing serve as a reminder of how far you have come. You are aware that time is forging on and it is a new period in your life. Nothing stays the same and you must move with this shift in the right spirit.

Archangel Ariel works with you on obtaining material success. She knows that as a human soul, you have a need for certain material necessities. This isn't to be confused with a greedy hunger for material excess. She provides abundance by showering it upon you when you ask her to work with you in your life.

Ariel is ever present in all nature settings, high up in our mountains, soaring along with the wind in the deserts and surfing the waves of the oceans. Your concrete material needs increase when you invite Archangel Ariel into your life and follow her guidance. Success is not always financial. It can also be a state of mind in feeling grateful and optimistic with where you are at now and how far you have come. Be grateful for what you currently have. See the blessings that you have in your life right now. Do not think about or worry over what is coming next or what is not here. Put that all aside and let loose, enjoy yourself, celebrate and have a good time. Living in the moment and enjoying it brings you closer to having your dreams come true since positive thoughts attract the same energy to you.

There is nothing wrong with believing in yourself and shouting what you have accomplished from the highest mountain. Graciously accept all positive gifts showered upon you and do it without guilt.

Ariel also asks that you make regular efforts to connect with family or close ones. When we say family, know that it does not necessarily mean your earthly blood related family. Family is a place of unity, hope and gatherings with like minded souls. Families are your friends, your close ones, the trusted ones. We are all family and connected as souls.

Ariel shows me vibrant images of people boldly wearing warm, bright colors to accentuate their state of being. They are outdoors basking under a beautiful warm day. Their personalities are rich with fulfillment. They bask in smiles and are having a good time. They are not gossiping or speaking negative words. They are laughing while feeling joy and relaxation. This is what Ariel wants for you. She wants to help you get to that place of being in this state around the clock. Get outside and rejoice in a private celebration known only to your soul. Call up a friend who knows how to have a good time. Let all of your cares go and have an awesome time in this life!

Mother Nature is the perfect place for spiritual and personal enrichment of the body and soul. There are more angels, guardians and spirits watching over every flower, every grass, rock, mountain terrain than anywhere else in the world. Ariel rules the nature areas with her strong Earthly spirit presence. Many human souls stick close to other people in the bigger cities. This is where most of the negative energy is. This is where there is an immense amount of people, buildings, or man-made developments.

No matter what you are facing, Ariel can help toughen your inner self's resolve. Pull yourself up by your bootstraps and run over your challenges with great vigor and detachment. Take the rough patches in your life with stride. Being strong can be difficult when you are facing adversity. You can be strong by taking control of you and your life. Accept that some things have happened beyond your control and leave it alone. Know that it is all for a reason even if you cannot see the reason immediately. Ariel will help you be the calm within the storm. You handle your challenges the way Ariel tames the beast and lion. This is done with assertive grace.

# Messages from Archangel Haniel

Archangel Haniel works overtime during the week of the Full Moon transit which happens once a month. The intensity pull of the Full Moon begins to build 3-5 days before the day of the Full Moon and then 3-5 days afterwards. It affects so many at once which is why Archangel Haniel's work runs full time during that transit. The Full Moon can make one feel uncomfortable while bringing up feelings of anxiety, uneasiness, stress and depression. It places a spotlight on what you are going through internally and pulls that out of you for you and those around you to see. Because it brings that stuff out, some souls may be prone to want to cover up those prickly feelings with toxic substances or addictions to cope. This will not make it go away, but instead will mask the cut like a band aid. You will wake up the next day feeling low again.

If there is anything negative lurking within you, then examine what it is and then release it. Some do this through Full Moon rituals. You cannot make a mistake when you are purging something under a Full Moon. It is about setting the intention that you want to get rid of whatever baggage or emotion you have been carrying around. Intention is feeling what you want with every fiber of your being. You feel it in your mind, your heart and your stomach. Many use the night of the Full Moon to purge this baggage, because the energy of the Full Moon is incredibly powerful. You may want to make a list of the things you would like to get rid of on a piece of paper. On the night of the Full Moon, say each line mentally or out loud. Follow this by releasing it to Heaven. You can release it by mentally releasing it, by shredding the list, and then tossing it in the trash or burning it safely.

The Full Moon tends to prompt the ego to shout their issues into the ethers or to anyone who will listen. The Full Moon loves drama and puts all of it out there on display. You want to be extra cautious that you do not express every single emotion that could cause some backfiring where personal relationships are concerned. If you are angry or irritated about something, wait until the Full Moon passes before acting if you can help it. I've noticed so many ignore this advice unable to control themselves. They eventually witness it backfire. They end up worse off than they were before.

The Full Moon brings up anguish, anxiety and fears. All of that is a mirage, but the energy pull of the Full Moon aggravates your inner emotions lodged within you. Thoughts produce things so if you are marinating in constant daily worry over an issue, then that will expand and bring more of that to you around the Full Moon time. Release negative thoughts and get rid of it. It does not do you or anybody any good to hang onto that stuff. The thoughts are so powerful that you refuse to let them go. This is a burden of heavy weight on your soul, which can stall you from movement. It essentially holds you prisoner.

The Full Moon energy pushes you to fall deep into your psyche. It pulls out your most troubled issues in order for you to address, release or correct the issue. Imagine the plaguing thoughts are sitting in your hand. Cup your hands together and lift them into the air. Follow this by opening up your hands allowing the troubles you have gathered up to fly out into the air up towards Heaven for transmutation. Perform this with intention and you are heard. Once completed, feel the release all throughout your body. Your spirit and light will expand upward to a higher level. You will look back in hindsight wondering why you were holding onto those negative thoughts, people and circumstances so tightly.

When you are riding on a level of joy, the answers or insights you need miraculously appear. Archangel Haniel relays these insights to you. She heightens your psychic perception so that you receive profound insights that can benefit you in a positive way.

There is often talk about the dark energies in the world, but Haniel says your soul must meet challenges in this lifetime. This is how you grow, change and evolve to the next plateau. However, these challenges do not have to be difficult or seen as dark. It is all in how your mind perceives them to be. As long as you remain grounded, centered and keep an optimistic attitude, then you will be fine. You will be able to handle the challenges that come your way with poise.

Archangel Haniel works hard during any Full Moon week helping you have deep insight while awakening your own inner truth. During the Full Moon, your emotions will increase. This might make one cry out for help. Haniel hears these cries and moves into your space to ease you of any pain you're experiencing. The Full Moon and Haniel combined open up your intuition and sixth sense. It is important to understand the difference between what heavenly prophecy is and what your fears and ego are. The Full Moon energy unleashes all of that intertwined with one another so it might cause confusion. Ask Haniel to give you crystal clear signs of what you are intended to know. She asks you to remain positive as you purge and release any negativity in your life. As you release these things to Heaven and the Universe, be optimistic knowing that they will go through a transmutation process and in return bring you blessings.

When you work with Archangel Haniel, she reveals hidden truths and secrets. Some of this guidance can be the information you need to reap rewards from your endeavors and ideas. She shines a light on this truth. This may cause upset, as it is sometimes not expected or wanted news. The truth reveals itself so that you do not continue living in denial. Denial cripples your soul's growth and movement.

You might be shown people or circumstances who should not be in your life to begin with and you have to face this truth. Ultimately, what follows is a positive transformation related to your growth. Those that will get through it effortlessly are those who already do the emotional work on a regular basis. Haniel holds a mirror up to your inner emotions and world. She does not allow anything to stay bottled up.

Archangel Haniel awakens psychic perception and unleashes emotional issues you might have buried deep within. She assists you with purging this while discovering hidden secrets about yourself or someone else. Perhaps you have found out that someone you are personally involved with on some level has not been operating with integrity. Before jumping to conclusions, it is important to address any issues with them by communicating peacefully about it. Remember that not all may be what it appears during a Full Moon transit. If you find that this person is repeatedly hostile or defensive when you attempt to have a healthy discussion, then this might be a sign to distance yourself from them if even temporarily.

The energy of the Full Moon is so intense and powerful that some souls cast important spells during this transit. Spells have two important ingredients: Energy and intention. Intention is feeling what you want in every cell of your body. When you put intention into a spell casting, then you are adding more energy into manifesting that which you are seeking. A spell merely enhances the energy of what you want. This is why it is important to be careful when working with energy. You are made up of energy and there can be repercussions with how you direct this energy. When in an angry mood about a situation, you'll find more negativity piles into your life. How many times has this happened and you have said, "Wow it's just one thing after another today?" You create your reality with your emotions and thoughts.

You do not need to have a spell cast to work with intention. Meditate on the Full Moon and commune quietly with Archangel Haniel about what you desire. Create your own ambient sanctuary with candles, incense, and soft music playing. Write down a list of what you would like to release and then burn it or trash it. Let it go and follow this with what you do want. This does not have to be material items. This can be requesting that you have a more positive mindset. It can be that you do not hold grudges towards others so intensely and are able to forgive more readily. Since you manifest from within, fixing your inner self will assist you in bringing grand opportunities much more swiftly to you. Having an optimistic attitude, and being able to forgive and forge on, will keep your manifestations positive.

It is important to remain affirmative during this process. Recite positive statements to remind your soul of the good that is around you. Say what you want with intention, but say it as if you already have it and that it is here in your life now. List the things and people you want to release. *(i.e., thank you for releasing my anger, thank you for releasing my fears, etc.)*

Check the calendar for the Full Moon dates of the year. Call in Archangel Haniel to work with you then in releasing toxic energy, people and substances. Be open to letting go of all that no longer serves your higher good, then be receptive to the blessings that will follow.

# Messages from Archangel Azrael

Archangel Azrael is with those grieving, in distress, or experiencing loss. He helps you unburden the load of heavy emotions associated with any kind of ending that brings turmoil, especially the death of a loved one. He guides and assists the souls who cross over to the other side, as well as the human souls on Earth experiencing a major transition in their life. Azrael is present whenever there is a crucial soul transition in one's life. Major transitions and transformations can cause prolonged suffering when not attended to. Azrael eases your soul allowing the crossroads one is moving through to happen more efficiently than without his help.

Endings can be anything from friendships and relationships, to eliminating harmful lifestyle choices. They can be circumstances that no longer operate in your life. This can be work related endeavors or relationships. Many experience uncomfortable feelings on some level or inner turmoil during a transition or ending.

Your soul wakes up when faced with the death of a close loved one. You come to terms with your own mortality and see the rest of the world and its way of life as being trivial and superficial. Circumstances open up in profound ways after the death of a loved one, even though this might not be evident right away.

Some soul's crossing over fear the light and might avoid moving through it. They equate the light with judgment or eternal Hell. This is due to their upbringing on Earth with others hammering into their psyches that there is a wrath of judgment waiting for them. This is not based in the reality of what happens when you cross over. This is discussed in a chapter in my book, *Warrior of Light: Messages from my Guides and Angels*. Your ego, feelings and thoughts remain whole as you cross over. They are no longer confined and trapped within the heavy weight of the human body. If your soul stays on the Earth's plane instead of moving graciously into the light, then you will continue to cling to the negative traits you assumed while in a human body. However, if you let go of this control and move with the natural process of crossing over to the other side, you will gradually feel any pain lifted off your soul. You will retain this information in your subconscious and pull it out when it is your time to cross over.

Many human souls are battling intense energies and emotions as we move out of the final Dark Age. With this comes tons of purging and releasing of the old ways of living that no longer work for you. There are human souls rigidly stuck in the dark ages. Azrael helps you along as you move through an indefinite closure to a situation or way of life that must end. Closure or completion is a reason to celebrate as it moves you to the next plateau of your soul's growth. Enjoy the rewards that come with the effort or lessons you have gained through this completion. It is a transition into something far greater.

There comes a time in your life where you will experience an ending that you're unprepared for. This might have happened already at least once in your life. A door closes on a chapter that your ego does not want to end. You are moving down another path which feels unknown. This may conjure up something unpleasant within you. Call on Archangel Azrael to be your guide and protector to have with you on this important ride, such as an event that requires closure. Perhaps your love relationship has ended abruptly and you feel devastation and depression. Maybe you are experiencing wasted emotions in your relationship, such as plaguing thoughts of suspicion or jealousy. It is driving you mad, but you do not know how to stop it on your own. You feel like an unattached leaf blowing in the wind without the security you had come to know while in this relationship. Azrael is the powerful being you will want to invite into your life to help you through it much more quickly.

This can be any kind of ending beyond a relationship. It can be an actual death of a loved one, the ending of a job and the beginning of a new one. It can be a transition into another life, or if you're feeling stuck in limbo. Azrael is the Archangel Light who smoothes out the rough edges and helps ease any feelings of sadness, depression or confusion. He will brighten up your world just when you need it most.

Azrael is there for a death or ending whether physical or metamorphic. Death is nothing to fear. The word has a negative connotation to it, but death is the opportunity to move into something more incredible beyond what you can imagine. It is the ending of one way of life and the ushering in of a newer more improved one. It feels like everything is over, but this is an illusion. What is happening is opportunity. What once existed has now run its course. The pain that endured on any level must be stopped. When it reaches its end, then you can be free. Call in Archangel Azrael to assist with any transition in your life. You will find that circumstances start working itself out. You will reach a happier and content space much more rapidly.

# Messages from Archangel Metatron

Archangel Metatron focuses his light on the new souls being born. These young people are entering a new phase in their soul's growth and he is here to assist them on their journey. Remain optimistic and open as you navigate the choppy waters that this life hands you at times. Children are born wide-eyed with a clean slate and not tampered with by the human ego of others. Do not allow others to influence you in a negative way. This is your life and you need to live it for you. Focus on all of the opportunities and possibilities that await you. This applies to anyone who is about to embark on a new chapter in their life. In this state, you are also open to whatever circumstances come your way. Be carefree and detached from all negativity, stresses and worries. You have the entire world at your feet as you forge on a new path with no baggage. You have nothing to lose and are ready to seize fresh opportunities. Being in the right space is by feeling excitement and optimism. This can be the young adult heading off to college with immense anticipation, or it can be someone who moves into a new home with the intention of starting a healthy, positive life. They all have a blank canvas to paint their newly gained knowledge onto.

I have been living several lifetimes rolled into this one particular lifetime. With that have come many forks in the roads. These have been transitions, awakenings and spiritual evolutions. If you have reached at least one major transition in your life, then you can be sure that Archangel Metatron is present around you. The awakenings we speak of are the kind of transitions that propel you into something profoundly empowering. Metatron takes immediate note when he sees human souls with a clear road ahead of them. He sees that these souls are looking to improve themselves. He swoops in brightening up the way leading them out of any previous darkness. He assists those souls by helping them live in the moment and enjoy what their new life has to offer. Believe, trust and have faith in the miracles that he bestows upon you as you forge down a sunnier road with a brighter outlook.

Move through life as if you have the world at your feet. This broadens your vision and the Heavenly guidance becomes clearer. You take chances on things that you ordinarily would not have done before you propelled forward with this new life. These chance circumstances are positive opportunities and not to be confused with experimenting with toxic ways of living that includes drugs, alcohol and partying, etc. Those are escapism tendencies, which offer no positive benefit in the end. There is nothing wrong with having a drink once in awhile. Heaven says this only for your benefit. They know that the great high you crave is when you are operating from your higher self and free of toxic vices and addictions. Your mind is clearer and your perception is broader.

You cannot sit back and allow your dreams and opportunities to come to you without effort. You need enormous willpower and determination to reach the varying heights of success. Metatron guides these particular souls down these new roads. His focus is on those souls who put in the work. It is not enough to embark on a new journey with no point or destination in sight. The souls highlighted are the ones who have a spark ignited within them. They have a thirst for knowledge wanting to accomplish many positive things while here. They have strength of will and drive. They are good people and their resolve brings them to enormous heights. Even in the face of setbacks, they do not allow that to crush their spirit or depress them. They brush it off as if it is merely a little bit of dust on their shoulder. They continue smiling while remaining open as they proceed on to the next step. They do not see the disappointments as anything remotely strong enough to stop them on their quest. Instead, they are inspired and ready for the next challenge. There will be struggles, but this soul knows there are more victories that supersede that. In the end, the efforts are worth it. When you do the work in evolving your spirit, the wonders and triumphs gained in your life overpower any menial setbacks. Archangel Metatron plays an important part in this process for these particular souls.

# Messages from Archangel Sandalphon

Archangel Sandalphon says that there are divinely guided artists in front of all of us. These include singers, musicians, painters, photographers, comedians, entertainers to actors, writers and anyone in the creative arts. He sends a reminder that if a human ego chooses to dislike an artist, then they must remember that the artist is a light of god. The artist has a purpose that benefits and attracts in specific human souls for a reason. Everyone is in various stages of awareness and development. Not all human souls love the same artist, but you must respect all of God's creation regardless. Those who are in the arts have varying purposes that inspire, uplift or change someone's way of thinking into something more positive. They may not motivate or attract you, but they do attract in someone who needs their inspiration to be empowered. These artists, actors, musicians and writers have a role in this lifetime that benefits others in a positive way. They are able to lift the vibrations of other human souls simply through their inspired creative work. This work is heavenly guided and Archangel Sandalphon is at the helms running the show like a conductor with an orchestra.

Archangel Sandalphon is the muse who channels God's light through the human souls that entertain and create. He also does this with healers and spiritual teachers as well. Archangel Sandalphon is a bit of a traditionalist. There are artists out there who entertain and bring joy to the masses.

They should not be confused with the artists who shock for mere attention and ego gratifying purposes. The artists all have elements of divinely guided work within them. Mixed with this is the tug of war of the ego. This is due to the demands of promoting and selling your art as a business. In the end, they serve the purpose of entertainer and heavenly inspiration, even though on occasion their ego may run the show. The basic light and concept within each of their souls is profound.

Sandalphon was a holy man when he was a human soul and this energy magnified as an Archangel. Because he can be with as many as he wants to be, his role carries over to the spiritually wise. This is from those who work in the church to those who are spiritual healers on any level. His light is around the schools, learning institutions, self-help organizations of all types. This is by acting as a holy teacher. He guides or inspires those in the teaching professions towards the right road where they can benefit the masses positively. Some human souls abuse their gifts and operate from massive ego, so it is important to note the difference between what is divinely inspired and what is not. The ego of a human soul never listens to the guidance and messages of any enlightened heavenly soul and spirit. When an artist or teacher is not operating from their higher self, they are experiencing their own lessons and repercussions as a human soul by their personal actions. This has nothing to do with the real work put out there when they function from their true self.

# Messages from Archangel Raguel

Archangel Raguel shifts your perspective towards one that is fair, balanced and objective. This reduces friction, pain, or any other unpleasant emotion that rises during a rift with another party or person. Raguel is all about compromise. Hanging dangerously close to the middle is always best. It benefits all parties especially when experiencing a disagreement. Archangel Raguel points out that so many human souls have a detachment from God and spirit. This is evident in the way that souls have a hyper rigid view with no room for movement. If someone does not believe in the same things they do, then they attack them. In some instances they kill them!

As any intelligent being can point out, having no room for compromise does not bring people together. This is evident in media, politics and religion. Three circumstances which control and develop human souls. Your ego wants to dominate and it is stubborn, rigid and bruised when slighted. It acts out in aggression or in upset when something does not go according to its plan. Your higher self and soul are too high up to be bothered with such pettiness. Your higher self is unaffected by slights done to it. It knows that others are acting out of ego and this warrants no attention. It stands strong like a lone reed in the wind. This applies to all connections when it reaches a place of tension or discord. This is when you should immediately call in Archangel Raguel to smooth out the rough edges and bring balance and fairness to all parties involved.

The problem is when confronted with antagonism by another, your ego immediately slams on the gas without thinking anything through. It runs over everything in its way like a car driving out of control. It knocks things out of the way with aggression only to find you've gained nothing in the end. The only thing gained is angry emotions which cause further internal and external harm. Your ego has control and does not listen to the voice of God or your higher self. It becomes a naughty, spoiled child throwing a tantrum. What happens when a child behaves this way? A proper parent trains the child by sending them away to their room. They withhold the activities the child enjoys. The child does not get any of the wonderful prizes. Taken away from them are the toys or video games they love. The parent sends them away ignoring them and leaving them left to sulk and pout. No one pays much attention to a child stomping their feet and acting out. In addition, neither does any adult when there is conflict. You are only thinking for yourself in those instances. This is where Archangel Raguel comes in to dissolve those cords of strife. When you request his intervention he brings peace and harmony to all parties involved. If you do not wish the one you are angry with to receive harmony in a disagreement, then you will not receive it either.

Archangel Raguel is beneficial for couples who are distant and no longer connecting. He can lift the thorns of distance or disagreement and help the couple to find compromise and middle ground. What happens afterwards is the couple begins working together and meeting each other half way. Raguel nudges them to open up peacefully and lovingly with one another. Neither of them understands where the immediate camaraderie has come from, unless they work with Raguel firsthand. This also carries over to legal drama or issues with particular organizations where they are exerting their power and intimidation over you. Call in

Archangel Raguel immediately to help the situation and bring a positive conclusion for all parties. Archangel Raguel would make an awesome right hand man for anyone who is an attorney or practices law. It cannot hurt you or your cases when you request that he works with you full time.

There is no doubt that many human souls are in relationships where there is no communication. They have built up tension, estrangement or arguments. Speak your mind lovingly and work it out together in order to bring any misunderstandings to closure. Addressing issues allows you to start a new chapter in your life with this person. The illusions and deceptions going on within certain relationships are an interesting dichotomy. There will be secrets that pop up or new discoveries you wish you had not known about. Some of your thoughts may be deceptive by exaggerating a situation. This is where your relationship appears one way and you jump to conclusions about it only to discover it was not true. You say, "Oh was that all it was." Some of the thoughts you conjure up can be detrimental causing a potential break up or add hostility to your union. When you allow negative thoughts about what you think your partner is doing to overtake you, then it's time to bring in Archangel Raguel. He will infuse harmony within your relationship, or a peaceful separation if it has been abusive.

How Raguel works is he helps all parties involved have an eagle's eye view of how they are playing a part in the friction. If you are with a love partner that contributes nothing to the relationship, then Raguel can help bring in a love partner who is balanced and in the relationship with you. He will not do this without first nudging your partner to make significant changes in how they invest or contribute towards the relationship. Since you have free will, some souls will ignore his guidance. If this is the case where both parties are unwilling to bend from their innate values and put in an effort, then Raguel will dissolve the union and bring another soul mate potential into your life that is more aligned with your beliefs and ways of living. However it is important to note that if you're someone who is inflexible to begin with, and you place excessive and outlandish demands on your partner, then you may end up alone. No high vibrational potential soul mate will put up with a controlling disciplinarian for a love partner, let alone be attracted to it to begin with. Give yourself a good hard objective look to see where you play a part in relationship friction. If you're unable to, then ask a close trusted one to be honest with you about your basic behavior in general and in relationships. Be prepared for the answer and work on those negative traits about you that need to be adjusted so that you can attract in a loving soul mate partner.

When you are with someone in a love relationship who does not know what they want, then this creates an imbalance between the both of you. This can be where you are more committed to the relationship than they are. This can also be relationships where neither party works on the connection together by opening up and communicating regularly. Both parties are affected negatively by the lopsided energy moving back and forth between you. You block abundance and great things in your life when there is an imbalance such as this. Call on Archangel Raguel to work with you on your relationship if this is the case. Ask him for guidance if you do not know what to do. Step out of the way and pay attention to any repeated signs he gives you.

You know you do not want to leave the love relationship, but you know it cannot continue in its current state. This is where Raguel can work his magic and help you both find a common ground using compromise. Compromise means both parties will need to let go of certain rigid beliefs so that you are on an equal level. Compromising is considering your partner's feelings. It is meeting them half way with issues so that you can both be happy. Both of you need to do this. This is not to say that you have to deny who you are, but you do need to be clear with each other. You have to be willing to work on the areas that cause unhappiness within the union. If one or the both of you is unable or unwilling to, then the relationship will either end or continue the way it is indefinitely.

If you are with someone who never knows what they want when it comes to your connection, then ask Archangel Raguel to intervene and help correct this indecisiveness. He will do this by bringing you together, or by bringing in someone aligned with your relationship values. This would be someone who wants to commit to you and knows this without a doubt. Raguel knows for sure that the person you are with will never want the things you want. Archangel Raguel, like all heavenly hosts, is profoundly psychic and knows what you and your mate desires even if neither of you says it to one another. Raguel clairvoyantly sees that your partner will be more committed to you years down the line. He may ask you to be patient as he avoids bringing you someone new, because he knows that all will be well with your current mate eventually.

# Messages from Archangel Chamuel

Everyone has more than one soul mate in their lifetime. Soul mates are not just love relationships. They can be friends, family members, business connections, lovers, animals, acquaintances and even your own Children. It can be someone in passing that relays information to you that shifts your world towards something brighter. Soul mates challenge you and open you up. They help you face your baggage and learn from your mistakes. They help your spirit grow and enhance. This Earthly life is one big class after all. This is what it means when someone says that the person you're dating would be good for you.

Archangel Chamuel understands this human need for a love partner. Therefore, he works diligently to bring many human souls together in loving relationships when they request his help. He can also work on your current relationship connections, and with those relationships from the past that ended without closure. If you have found people popping up from your past to re-connect, know that they are appearing for a reason that benefits your soul. You might feel uncomfortable with that and throw your hands in the air, "Oh I'm not talking to them!" The re-connection is to give you or them an opportunity to have closure. You need to make your peace with them. This is by forgiving them for what they might have done to hurt you. You do this when you allow them back into the picture to make amends and balance your connection out. You do not have to continue with a forged friendship or relationship with them, but there is previous Karma that needs working on between the two of you. Chamuel says that this is going back to make good with what was wronged in the past.

I have been with those who are all brains. They have little to no emotion, feeling or love. Meanwhile, I am feeling drained with all of my giving stuff. I sensed the great imbalance in those connections. On top of that, my soul feels neglected on other levels since I crave a high quotient of romance and passion on a regular basis. Each of your relationship connections prep you to work on certain things pertaining to your soul. You have insight to gain while in them.

In this modern day world, it can be rare to see a couple go the distance. Part of this is due to the many contributing factors that exist today. The ego is powerful wanting to be free. It finds it difficult to merge comfortably and unconditionally with others. Chamuel can assist you in opening up your heart to love by stripping away your obsession with what your ego demands in a love relationship. He can bring you a new sense of self and help you love yourself more. When you love you, then you attract in a wonderful loving mate into your life that picks up on your high vibration. People are turned off and not attracted to someone who exudes a consistent dose of insecure feelings. I was involved with someone such as this. It ultimately ended at the hands of the insecure one who placed me on too high of a pedestal. They ultimately felt as if they could not measure up and also preferred to be free and unattached.

Chamuel will bring you a new partner or a renewed passionate feeling with your current partner if this is what you choose. He will help you experience a deeper connection with each other. In my particular case I understood that Chamuel was dealing with someone who governed their life primarily from free will and ego. Archangel Chamuel also prompts marriage proposals or stronger commitments between two souls. He will bring in a new beginning in your relationship where it feels you are starting a brand new relationship with the same person. This can be in a current relationship or just a renewed outlook on how you would want your relationship to be. These relationships always include love, friendships, neighbors, families, business colleagues...you name it. It all applies and Chamuel wants to assist to bring you more love and harmony in your life. This raises your vibration which ultimately helps the energy on the planet. When you have joyful and peaceful human souls, you have a high vibrational energy wave that affects the globe. This is why the Archangels work with you on the little things to get you happy!

Archangel Chamuel helps you examine the connections you have with others. The ties you make with other people whether they are a lover, friend, colleague, boss, sibling, parent or even child are no accident. You have bonds with certain souls where you feel like you are being tested at times. Perhaps every time you are with this person you feel uncomfortable or you feel forced to put on the face and be civil to avoid a disagreement. Chamuel asks that you look at the unions that cause you some form of upset or grief. Observe the underlying lessons within them. Make your peace with it and then let it go. This can also be a circumstance where you are drawn to the same type of wrong person repeatedly. You cannot seem to let them go even though you are perfectly aware they are damaging to you. There are a couple of reasons for this. One of them is that you both have unfinished lessons together. Each person needs the characteristics that the other has in order to fulfill a specific lesson. This will help in their spiritual growth while here. Once the lessons are learned and you have changed positively because of it, then the shift happens and you attract in healthier, stronger people into your life.

An example of a scenario is a guy who came from an abusive household. With him is his girlfriend who is a successful, self-confident and well-respected human soul in her career. They meet and are immediately attracted to one another and thus form a relationship. Over time, she loses herself in the relationship. Feeling the imbalance she starts to assert herself, as this is how she used to be before the relationship. When she does this though, he cuts her down using the violence and bullying he learned from his upbringing. He continues to belittle and cut her down. She starts to believe it and ultimately leaves him. Yet, he comes around apologizing and begging for forgiveness. She is drawn right back to him again as she remembers all the good times and forgets about the violence. The lesson here for both of them to learn is that he needs to stop the cycle of violence in his family history, and she needs to learn to assert herself and not falter once in a relationship. Someone will love all of who she is without compromise.

There are lessons in all of your connections that you must learn in order for you to grow. If this does not happen, you will continue to attract in the same types of people who exude similar characteristics from one another. You are essentially attracted to these types of people without realizing it until you are knee deep in it.

How often do you hear someone say, "Why do I keep attracting the same types of people to me?" It is important to come to terms with the lesson you are meant to learn in how or why you are attracting in the same characters. These connections are not happening by chance. Once you have honed in on this, then it is time to enact an inner change. This is in order to start attracting in relationships at a higher level. It is common to be unaware that there is a lesson in these unions while you are in them. Your ego and lower self takes over and places blame on the other person. It looks at what the other person is doing to them. This is giving your power away to someone else. You need to take a step back to see the lesson you must learn in that particular relationship that will prompt you to grow and move to the next level. Once you have done that, you experience a release from that tie. You will attract in souls who are nothing like who you used to be attracting in. You will instead invite in new, healthier relationships and connections.

# Messages from Archangel Zadkiel

Archangel Zadkiel restores balance in your life and helps you find peace. He brings your life to a place where you are giving and dispersing equal energy towards all that exists around you. This is from family, love, career and home. He knows that when one area is lopsided that you feel out of sorts. You become distressed, worn and agitated. To reach a place of peace is to accept that your needs happen on their own course and time. Zadkiel can help you be at peace with how your life is. He will guide you to live in the now by exercising patience with what is to come.

Zadkiel guides you away from excess. This includes whatever you are abusing or addicted to. If you have been consuming too much alcohol for example, then he can diminish this need when you ask for his intervention.

What is important is seeing all sides of an equation or argument with an objective view. Zadkiel helps you stay neutral because taking sides gets everyone nowhere. He helps you find the balance between opposing views and issues.

Unrequited is about anything that is not reciprocated. When there is no reciprocation in your life, then there is no balance. If you want to witness an investment, profit or return in terms of your desires, then button down the hatches and drive full force into your passion. Put all of your energy into it knowing that the rewards will come out of it on its own time. You could be sitting idly around waiting for a hand out, but this will never happen. You have to get up and dive into what you want. When you do that, then you are met more than half way. Meditate on what you want. This is by being still and allowing ideas to come forth on your next step. Many meditate and connect with the other side in a myriad of ways. I enjoy jumping into physical activity. This is climbing, jogging or walking through nature. This is where the big messages from spirit happen for me.

If you want to see something positive manifest out of your interests and passions, then you have to go after it. This can be a business venture or even a romantic partner. If you feel like something is not happening in your life in a particular area or you are not seeing any sort of abundance or return coming in, then there may be an imbalance at play. Zadkiel asks that you question how much work you are putting into what you want. Perhaps you have been slacking a bit or taking some time off from it. He reminds you that some effort needs to happen on your part. Traits like patience, forgiveness and cooperating with other people is vital in certain situations. Meeting others half way will take you far.

Ask Archangel Zadkiel to balance your life out in every way possible and in every area in all directions of time. He can bring you a renewed sense of self and positive feelings of well-being into your life. This brings in the great miracles you dream of. You have the power to be happy, to accomplish your dreams and to do whatever it is that you seek to do as long as it is aligned with love. This power is at your fingertips and has been since birth into this lifetime, so go for it, access it and utilize it it.

Forgiveness is one of the most difficult acts for human souls to do. Your ego can hold slights so close to your soul to the point where that toxic feeling festers and grows tampering with your psyche. Zadkiel can help you release this non-forgiveness. Holding onto it towards anyone is not healthy because the only person it hurts is you. It is understandable to have anger towards someone who has abused you or treated you unkindly; however, it is necessary to reach that place where you do forgive them. When you do not forgive someone and you hang onto that tightly, then you create blocks that prevent you from reaching a state of happiness. You are not saying what they did to you is okay and nor are you letting them off the hook. You are forgiving them for yourself and so that you can be freed of that pain. This is for you and your overall soul. You know how it feels to hold onto negative emotions like anger or sadness. This state feels horrible! It bogs you down and you are unable to focus clearly. You end up making mistakes and you alienate people who care about you in the process.

Make a list in a notebook of those that you harbor resentment towards and why. Go over each line and mentally or out loud forgive them for the sake of release. Feel the heavy weight of not forgiving you carry, and then allow Archangel Zadkiel to transport it away to Heaven. Take that sheet of paper out of your notebook and destroy it in the name of God. This will release it and the energy.

Archangel Zadkiel aligns my vibration with those in the higher realms when I'm in the zone or channel. At times I cut in and out of frequency when important information or guidance is being relayed. It is Zadkiel that comes in and restores the communication line ensuring that it is crystal clear and connected. He's not someone I had originally called in to work with, but this was how he first introduced himself to me. Instantly he went into work mode whenever I moved into the channel space. He voluntarily comes in to adjust my frequency so that I hear my Spirit team clearly. This is especially beneficial when attempting to reach God or those in a higher plane. The higher I need to reach, the more he shows up to bend these etheric light cords that appear much like a telephone wire. The only difference is these are various different sparkly colored lights that bend, curve and distort depending on where my thoughts are. He is also brushing away dust, dirt and dark particles that sometimes accumulate around this wire.

Zadkiel is not around much on day-to-day communications with my Spirit team, but when I'm writing Spirit messages for a book for example, he is present through the entire process. Without my request, he shows up almost as if he wants to. This is no surprise that he keeps me connected since he works with clearing out the ear chakras. Your ear chakras are connected to your clairaudience. If I break out of the connection when vital messages are in the process of being relayed, then I will say, "Zadkiel, please connect me. Thank you." Thirty seconds to one minute later the connection is strong again. This is a common occurrence when it comes to the spiritual work. The many that are not around me regularly band together around me whenever I'm in work mode.

# Messages from Archangel Jeremiel

Martin Luther King Jr. was a warrior of light whose goal was peaceful activism in bringing people together. When he passed on into the next plane, it was intended that he be remembered on Earth for several things. One of them was to love and serve humanity. This is why all souls are here. See the innocence in someone's actions and release any harsh judgments that unknowingly plague you. Many are caught up in the past, worried about the future, and simultaneously trying to make huge transitions into a better life calmly. The ego is like a loud spoiled child and gets in the way by making you feel frustrated or confused. If you let it get a hold of you and run your life, then you will drown in its energy.

Jeremiel's message is to clear the clutter and space in and around you, from your mind, your place of work and even your car. All souls on Earth are transforming globally. Even if they are not aware of it, it is happening and has been for centuries. You can move with it graciously or have an outburst, which is what you might be witnessing in others who partake in violence, hate or cruel judgments. There is no going back to the past as it is outdated and no longer realistic. With this change comes seeing things in a new light. The way to transform into this new life is to start at the core individually. This is by organizing yourself, your surroundings, and your life one step at a time. Adopt healthy new ways of living and seeing circumstances. This includes releasing any feelings of guilt or sadness you carry around regarding someone or a past decision you made. Forgive yourself and others for previous mistakes you or they have made.

The colors of Archangel Jeremiel are a bright and vibrant violet color with indigo tinges. This light latches onto everything around you when he is present. The violet light is the light energy of physical and spiritual transformation. The way he works is by washing your soul as if it is experiencing a baptism. Allow his light to wash over you and clear away any debris which prevents you from moving forward. Get rid of all that senseless weight. Do not be afraid to get your feet wet as you release issues of the past. Call on Archangel Jeremiel who will work with you through this process using grace and willingness.

Clutter creates chaos and this is why it is important to do a routine stripping of any disorder in your surroundings. Archangel Jeremiel conducts a life review and part of this process is by removing things that no longer serve you once it's addressed. He has you examine your past with a fine toothcomb before you make your peace with it. You must make your peace with it before he releases it from your aura. Making your peace with it includes understanding why the situation happened to begin with. This will help you feel complete, whole and ready for your next juncture.

Learn from your circumstances, choices and experiences. If you are buried in heavy feelings in relation to what is not working in your life, then it is time to work through this to reach a place of contentment. It does not help you when you are focused on feeling yucky emotions. In order to work through them, you have to examine them and look for the underlying cause and message. What areas in your life are provoking you in a negative way? Those areas require a major change on your part. Ask Archangel Jeremiel for help with this and follow his guidance even if it is pushing you out of your element. Following his instructions will help you move to the next plateau. See only the love and lessons in your current experiences and make your peace with it.

The Mercury Retrograde cycle is a planetary transit that happens three times a year. It forces every individual human soul to pause, move within and evaluate all areas of their life. Those who do not understand the Mercury Retrograde cycle tend to battle with anxiety and stress while making one error after another. They vent frustration and do not understand that the transit prompts you to pause whether you like it or not. Mercury Retrograde is not going to wait for a company or corporation to get with the program of the Universe. Mercury Retrograde is God created while corporations are man created. You cannot win a battle with the universe, God, and spirit, no matter how powerful your man made company is.

Look up the more in depth meaning of the Mercury Retrograde transit online. Knowing the dates of the Mercury Retrograde in any given year will help you prepare and plan important dates outside of that if possible. The Mercury Retrograde transit is a terrific time to do a life review with Archangel Jeremiel, since it is all about going back to examine the past. Of course, you can have a life review at anytime you are ready. The Mercury Retrograde transit prompts you to go back and re-trace your steps. What better time to go back, review and re-examine everything in your past than during the Mercury Retrograde transit. Re-evaluate your life, where you are at and see what needs changing or eliminating. When Mercury moves direct, use that time to take action steps to make the necessary improvements in your life that came to light during the Mercury Retrograde transit. Doing a thorough life review with Archangel Jeremiel can take some time, because if you are not owning up to the mistakes you made, then you do not move past the review. For some, this life review can take years or an entire lifetime.

# Jesus and Mother Teresa

 Whether or not you are a fan of Jesus Christ, you cannot deny the impact he has had on humanity and the world. He is not an Archangel, but he does fall into the category of what some consider an Ascended Master. This makes some religious followers uncomfortable, but an Ascended Master is a spiritually enlightened being. Jesus is absolutely this and so much more regardless of the title you prefer to give him. His messages and intention are about all love and all healing. He is not about anger or judgment. He is not about living your life in stress or greed. He is all about the uplifting joyous kind of love. This is why he was sent to Earth in human form. It was to teach that and spread it around. No one is going to listen to a spirit being. If they did, then we would not have the drama that exists all around the world throughout history. This is why many souls come into the Earthly plane in human soul form. They do this to send heavenly reminders and do the work for the Light. There are millions of human souls wandering off their path and forgetting how to love. They have grown to be indefinitely lost with no hope in sight.

Jesus is not typically the light I call in, although he has come in to visit by connecting through my clair channels on occasion. Those are the moments where I feel the indescribable kind of love that does not exist on Earth. It is a powerful euphoric feeling. It's as if you're soaring and floating above the clouds with immense eternal joy.

Before I entered this Earthly plane, Jesus was one of the final spirits to approach me before I came to be this lifetime. He said that love would be what I would retain from the spirit world. He whispered in my ear, "Remember all that matters is love. You will forget at times, but you will find your way back to that essence. At that moment, you will remember who you are and the purpose of your agreement. *We* will immediately connect with you when you are born into a human body, but it will take some time before you fully remember."

He said I would be tested in unimaginable ways in order to know what human suffering was like. I watched others on Earth suffer while on the other side, but I felt nothing. I was detached, but this was a detachment with love and not a cold indifference. There are different levels in the way spirits feel and perceive things. As a warrior hunter on the other side, I had some measure of disconnection to the pain that human souls suffer through. All I knew and understood was taking care of business. I have incorporated that into my purpose here as a human soul.

## God Has a Plan For Me

Some have used the phrase: "God has a plan for me." There is some truth to this statement. Those who have used that phrase have forgotten that it is your plan too. You made the agreement with Him before your soul entered this life. You know what His and your plan is. It is up to you to discover what that is. No one can tell you what it is. It was removed from your memory bank on purpose so that you can stumble on your way to discovering this plan. If you did not stumble, you would not grow and evolve. What matters is how you glide over life's challenges and become a stronger soul because of it.

There is much selfishness, rebelliousness and ego on the

planet. This comes from those who are not seeing the real gifts that exist in their life. Count your blessings on a daily basis. The *'poor me'* or *'I wish things were different'*, way of thinking will only make you feel more stuck. It blocks positive manifestations and you dig an even deeper hole into a bottomless abyss.

## MOTHER TERESA

This huge burst of shining white light wanted to live in the trenches on Earth in order to make a difference. She never wavered from her quest, which was solely focused on reaching out to the poor, the hungry, and the destitute. Her light was so bright to begin with, that it gave them all hope. Tirelessly she forged on even when faced with doubts that God existed. As a human soul, she had at times forgotten where she came from. Visiting those that are ignored by the world, she witnessed the conditions they lived in and could not understand how God could abandon them. How could He not intervene and help them? She would only entertain this uncertainty once in awhile. When that happened, Jesus lifted her up each time she expressed reservations. It is understandable to feel like your fight is worthless. It may seem like you are at odds with the world, but what you are really doing is fulfilling your mission. Your human life is sometimes faced with challenges in the process towards your life purpose.

Known to human souls as Mother Teresa, she crossed over back home to the other side and works as an Ascended Master once again. She is now a guide for those who tirelessly work on their life purpose in ways that help many people. She's with those who express doubts of God and wanting to stop their mission from time to time. You can call on her to work with you when you feel like throwing in the towel and giving up on your quest. She will strengthen you as she has come through for me. She visits you to lift those qualms off your body making your soul strong and whole again, so that you can forge on as a warrior of light. She radiates a light of love so magnificent it would astound you. Her work continues on the other side, as it always has. This is to help those in need. She does not fall into ego and instead adopts the mantra that all of Heaven lives in, which is pure love and joy. When Mother Teresa, also known as Agnes, came into an Earthly life, she immediately got to work and did not waste any time absorbing pettiness. She was on a mission that would carry on throughout her entire life and beyond.

What have you done lately? Do not forget who you are and why you are here. Never give up or throw in the towel. Forge on with your purpose and mission. Life on Earth is always critical due to the overpowering domination of the Devil, the Ego, and the lower self. They wrap themselves up into one and exist within you. The ignorance and blindness of the cancer can no longer be. Stomp out all of that darkness within and around you. Remember to love and fight in the name of the light.

Every human soul is born 100% psychic. These profound psychic gifts dim and nearly burn out once society, your peer, surroundings and the material world dominate and influence you. They train you to feel fear, stress, hate, guilt and low self esteem. All of this blocks communication from the other side. The psychic gifts that everyone has vary. For example, the other side communicates with you through one or more of the four major clairs that exist within your aura.

Your main clairs are Clairvoyance (Clear Seeing), Clairaudience (Clear Hearing), Clairsentience (Clear Feeling), Claircognizance (Clear Knowing). Usually two of the clairs are most dominant in you. I have heightened clairaudience, claircognizance, with some clairsentience and little clairvoyance. All of your clair channels can be opened or redeveloped, but it takes discipline and a lifestyle change.

When you allow yourself to be mired deeply in the ego, your lower self and material world, then your soul grows heavier and denser blocking out heavenly communication. These negative traits are on par with the Earth's atmosphere. When you remember who you are when you were born, and who you were when in the spirit world, only then do you come to terms with your own mortality. When you connect with the truth that you are a soul renting the body it inhabits, then the REAL reality and the bigger picture sinks in. When you experience any negative thoughts or emotions, be sure to call on your Spirit team of Guides and Angels to help restore your soul to optimum levels.

†

*Available in paperback and kindle by Kevin Hunter is the big spiritual handbook bible,*

## "WARRIOR OF LIGHT"
*Messages from my Guides and Angels"*

There are legions of angels, spirit guides, and departed loved ones in heaven that watch and guide you on your journey here on Earth. They are around to make your life easier and less stressful. Do you pay attention to the nudges, guidance, and messages given to you? There are many who live lives full of negativity and stress while trying to make ends meet. This can shake your faith as it leads you down paths of addictions, unhealthy life choices, and negative relationship connections. Learn how you can recognize the guidance of your own Spirit team of guides and angels around you.

Author, Kevin Hunter, relays heavenly guided messages about getting humanity, the world, and yourself into shape. He delivers the guidance passed onto him by his own Spirit team on how to fine tune your body, soul and raise your vibration. Doing this can help you gain hope and faith in your own life in order to start attracting in more abundance.

*Available in paperback and kindle by Kevin Hunter,*
## "REALM OF THE WISE ONE"

In the Spirit Worlds and the dimensions that exist, reside numerous kingdoms that house a plethora of Spirits that inhabit various forms. One of these tribes is called the Wise Ones, a darker breed in the spirit realm who often chooses to incarnate into a human body one lifetime after another for important purposes.

The *Realm of the Wise One* takes you on a magical journey to the spirit world where the Wise Ones dwell. This is followed with in-depth and detailed information on how to recognize a human soul who has incarnated from the Wise One Realm.

Author, Kevin Hunter, is a Wise One who uses the knowledge passed onto him by his Spirit team of Guides and Angels to relay the wisdom surrounding all things Wise One. He discusses the traits, purposes, gifts, roles, and personalities among other things that make up someone who is a Wise One.

Wise Ones have come in the guises of teachers, shaman, leaders, hunters, mediums, entertainers and others. *Realm of the Wise One* is an informational guide devoted to the tribe of the Wise Ones, both in human form and on the other side.

*Also available in paperback and kindle by Kevin Hunter,*

## "REACHING FOR THE WARRIOR WITHIN"

*Reaching for the Warrior Within* is the author's personal story recounting a volatile childhood. This led him to a path of addictions, anxiety and overindulgence in alcohol, drugs, cigarettes and destructive relationships. As a survival mechanism, he split into many different "selves". He credits turning his life around, not by therapy, but by simultaneously paying attention to the messages he has been receiving from his Spirit team in Heaven since birth.

**Kevin Hunter** gains strength, healing and direction with the help of his own team of guides and angels. Living vicariously through this inspiring story will enable you to distinguish when you have been assisted on your own life path. *Reaching for the Warrior Within* attests that anyone can change if they pay attention to their own inner guidance system and take action. This can be from being a victim of child abuse, or a drug and alcohol user, to going after the jobs and relationships you want. This powerful story is for those seeking motivation to change, alter and empower their life one day at a time.

Available in paperback and kindle by Kevin Hunter,
# "DARKNESS OF EGO"

The biggest cause of turmoil and conflict in one's life is executed by the human ego. All souls have an ego. The most unruly and destructive ego exists within every human soul. When the soul enters into a physical human body, the ego immediately compresses and then swells up. It is the higher self's goal to ensure that it remains in check while living an Earthly life.

The ego is what tests each soul along its journey. It is how one learns right from wrong. The experiences and challenges that the soul has while living in this Earthly life school contribute to the soul's growth. When a soul learns lessons, it is intended and expected to grow and enhance from the experience. Yet, there are a great many souls who do not learn lessons and remain in the same spot. The ill of the bunch wreaks all kinds of havoc, destruction, judgment and heart ache in its wake.

In *Darkness of Ego*, author Kevin Hunter infuses some of the guidance, messages, and wisdom he's received from his Spirit team surrounding all things ego related. The ego is one of the most damaging culprits in human life. Therefore it is essential to understand the nature of the beast in order to navigate gracefully out of it when it spins out of control. Some of the topics covered in *Darkness of Ego* are humanity's destruction, mass hysteria, karmic debt, and the power of the mind, heaven's gate, the ego's war on love and relationships, and much more.

The *Warrior of Light* series of mini-pocket books are available in paperback and E-book by Kevin Hunter called, *Spirit Guides and Angels, Soul Mates and Twin Flames, Divine Messages for Humanity, Raising Your Vibration, Connecting with the Archangels*

Also available in paperback and E-book by Kevin Hunter, *Ignite Your Inner Life Force*, *Awaken Your Creative Spirit* and *The Seven Deadly Sins*

# About Kevin Hunter

Kevin Hunter is an author, love expert and channeler. His books tackle a variety of genres and tend to have a strong male protagonist. The messages and themes he weaves in his work surround Spirit's own communications of love and respect which he channels and infuses into his writing and stories.

His books include the Warrior of Light series of books, *Warrior of Light*, *Empowering Spirit Wisdom*, *Realm of the Wise One*, *Reaching for the Warrior Within*, *Darkness of Ego*, *Ignite Your Inner Life Force*, *Awaken Your Creative Spirit* and *The Seven Deadly Sins*. He is also the author of the horror, drama, *Paint the Silence*, and the modern day erotic love story, *Jagger's Revolution*.

Before writing books and stories, Kevin started out in the entertainment business in 1996 becoming actress Michelle Pfeiffer's personal development dude for her boutique production company, Via Rosa Productions. She dissolved her company after several years and he made a move into coordinating film productions for the big studios on such films as *One Fine Day*, *A Thousand Acres*, *The Deep End of the Ocean*, *Crazy in Alabama*, *Original Sin*, *The Perfect Storm*, *Harry Potter & the Sorcerer's Stone*, *Dr. Dolittle 2* and *Carolina*. He considers himself a love addict and beach bum born and raised in Los Angeles, California.

Visit www.kevin-hunter.com

www.ingramcontent.com/pod-product-compliance
Lightning Source LLC
LaVergne TN
LVHW051118080426
835510LV00018B/2107